THE **MINI** ROUGH GUIDE TO

MAURITIUS
& RODRIGUES

YOUR TAILOR-MADE TRIP
STARTS HERE

Tailor-made trips and unique adventures crafted by local experts

HOW ROUGHGUIDES.COM/TRIPS WORKS

STEP 1

Pick your dream destination, tell us what you want and submit an enquiry.

STEP 2

Fill in a short form to tell your local expert about your dream trip and preferences.

STEP 3

Our local expert will craft your tailor-made itinerary. You'll be able to tweak and refine it until you're completely satisfied.

STEP 4

Book online with ease, pack your bags and enjoy the trip! Our local expert will be on hand 24/7 while you're on the road.

PLAN AND BOOK YOUR TRIP AT
ROUGHGUIDES.COM/TRIPS

HOW TO DOWNLOAD YOUR FREE EBOOK

1. Visit **www.roughguides.com/ free-ebook** or scan the **QR code** opposite

2. Enter the code **mauritius667**

3. Follow the simple step-by-step instructions

For troubleshooting contact: mail@roughguides.com

10 THINGS NOT TO MISS

1. **L'AVENTURE DU SUCRE MUSEUM**
   Get a taste of the island's sugar-producing heritage at this fascinating museum. See page 43.

2. **THE MAURITIUS RIVIERA**
   Take a trip to horseshoe-shaped Grand Baie for sandy coves, excursions and apres sol entertainment. See page 39.

3. **LA VALLÉE DE FERNEY**
   Its forests and trails beckon nature lovers. See page 46.

4. **BLACK RIVER GORGES NATIONAL PARK**
   Dramatic mountain vistas unfold. See page 50.

5. **GRIS GRIS**
   Huge waves crash against a wild coast. See page 58.

6. **CHAMAREL 7 COLOURED EARTH GEOPARK**
   This unusual geological phenomenon is the island's most visited site. See page 52.

7. **FRANÇOIS LEGUAT RESERVE RODRIGUES**
   See endemic plants and a colony of giant tortoises in Rodrigues. See page 80.

8. **ÎLE AUX CERFS**
   Clear waters off this island playground make for great snorkelling. See page 45.

9. **SIR SEEWOOSAGUR RAMGOOLAM BOTANIC GARDENS**
   An impressive showcase for tropical plants. See page 42.

10. **CHÂTEAU DE LABOURDONNAIS**
    A handsome colonial gem in a tropical garden setting. See page 37.

A PERFECT DAY

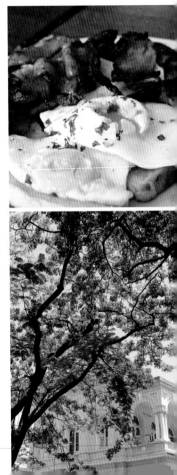

9am

Breakfast. Get off to a good start, away from the hustle and bustle of the city, with eggs Benedict and Mauritian coffee roasted on site at Bloom (tel: 230 268 3036, https://bloommauritius.com), a trendy eatery in Pereybere, before taking a fifteen-minute taxi ride to Port Louis.

10am

Green spaces. Walk off breakfast with a stroll through Company Gardens, see the Royal Palms in Place Sookdeo Bissoondoyal (previously Place d'Armes) leading up to Government House, or people-watch in Bowen Gardens.

12pm

Colonial chic. Take in the colonial architecture nearby, peek at the dodo skeleton in the Natural History Museum, then enjoy a light local lunch of *dholl puri* under the giant banyan trees in Company Gardens.

2pm

Retail therapy. Make your way to Trou Fanfaron and shop for souvenirs and samples of local dishes from the vendors. For fixed-price shopping, take the underpass to Le Caudan Waterfront and hit the Craft Market and scores of speciality and duty-free shops.

4pm

Stamp duty. Check out the Blue Penny Museum for famous portraits, fine art and philately. Cool off with a long drink on the terrace of the Labourdonnais Waterfront Hotel or head to the Food Court for fast food options.

IN **PORT LOUIS**

5.30pm

Sundowner. Take a free water taxi from the jetty car park across Bassin des Chaloupes to the trendy Pink Socks Bar at Le Suffren Hotel & Marina, order a New Grove rum cocktail, and catch a magnificent sunset from the terrace.

6.30pm

Dinner. Visit Le Courtyard, an elegant restaurant at the corner of St Louis and Chevreau streets (see page 109), with a shady terrace and a location in the heart of this bustling city. Taste fantastic dishes bursting with the flavours of France and Mauritius.

8.30pm

Bollywood versus Hollywood. Catch the latest English-subtitled Bollywood movies at MCine (tel: 230210 1900, https://mcine.mu) or settle in for a French-dubbed Hollywood blockbuster at the Star Cinema (tel: 230 211 6866) in Le Caudan Waterfront.

10pm

On the town. Try your luck at the casino's blackjack, roulette and poker tables or prop up the bar until the last punter leaves. Otherwise, plenty of taxis are on hand to take you north to the clubs and bars at Grand Baie. Best of the bunch is Banana Beach Club (tel: 230 263 0326, www.bananabeach club.com), a trusted hangout for live music by local jazz, rock and blues artistes, or follow the latest trend and head to a rooftop bar. The most impressive (and pricey) is Bisou at LUX Grand Baie (tel: 230 209 2200, www.luxresorts.com) with a swing over the infinity pool, which glows electric blue and pink at night (by reservation only).

CONTENTS

OVERVIEW

Mauritius has long entranced its visitors. Charles Baudelaire called it 'the perfumed land, fondled by the sun', while Mark Twain noted simply that 'heaven was copied after Mauritius'. The stunning white, sandy beaches lapped by aquamarine seas earn every superlative, and thousands of modern visitors to Mauritius agree that this tiny dot in the Indian Ocean is the stuff of desert-island dreams. With much of its coastline fringed by coral reefs, a landscape set off by diminutive mountains, temperatures rarely falling below 20°C (68°F) and some of the world's finest hotels, Mauritius is a perfect year-round holiday destination.

But there is more to Mauritius than the exclusive beachside hotels that have become the regular haunt of celebrities and big spenders. Stray inland and you will discover mountains, forests, rivers and waterfalls, fields undulating with sugar cane, extinct volcanic craters, tumbledown towns and villages and hospitable locals.

Mauritius lies 805km (500 miles) east of Madagascar, one of a trio of islands, along with Rodrigues and Réunion, known as the Mascarenes. Shaped like a pear, Mauritius covers an area of 1,865 sq km (720 sq miles). The island forms the main component of the Republic of Mauritius, which also includes the much smaller islands of Agaléga and St Brandon in the Cargados Carajos group and the autonomous island of Rodrigues.

There are three mountain ranges, courtesy of a volcanic past: the Moka Range forms an amphitheatre around the capital Port Louis; the Black River chain occupies the southwest, merging with the Savanne mountains in the extreme south; and the Grand Port Range lies in the southeast. Along the coast, the beaches, resorts and hotels of the north attract the majority of visitors; the

Rochester Falls

sheltered west, with its fantastic sunsets and access to rugged inland areas, is also popular; the east is isolated and rural but has some very luxurious hotels; there is a clutch of upmarket hotels in the 'green' southwest and a few in the sultry southeast, the last region to be developed.

THE PEOPLE

There are no indigenous people. The 1.3 million islanders are the descendants of enslaved Africans, indentured Indian labourers and Chinese traders, resulting in all shades of skin colour, a legacy of over three centuries of colonisation by the French and British. On this, one of the most densely populated islands on Earth, Indo-Mauritians form the majority at 68 percent, followed by Creoles or people of mixed European or African origin at 27 percent, Sino-Mauritians at 3 percent and white Franco-Mauritians at 2 percent. In Rodrigues, there are some 39,000 islanders, predominantly of

Creole-African descent. Most of the time, the republic's multicultural inhabitants get along in remarkable harmony.

Travelling round Mauritius reveals naturally friendly people who are keen to help visitors. Many live in the crowded plateau towns of Curepipe, Floreal, Rose Hill–Beau Bassin, and Quatre Bornes in the island's centre and small villages. It is here, and in the multicultural capital, Port Louis, that you discover the islanders' firm adherence to cultural traditions, witness religious festivals, taste a cuisine as diverse as its people and hear a multitude of different languages, including Creole, French, Hindi, Bhojpuri and, to a lesser degree, English, in an environment that contrasts strongly with the luxurious beach hotels and bustling tourist resorts of Grand Baie, Pereybere and Flic-en-Flac.

CREOLE

Creole is a language created by the need for French plantation masters to communicate with enslaved Africans and for the enslaved, who often spoke different dialects, to understand each other. Creole became the island's lingua franca. Continuously modified by years of French and English colonisation, Indian immigration and Chinese settlers, it has become a hopelessly corrupted language that often confuses Mauritians themselves. Full of imagery and nuances, it is slightly easier to understand if you have a basic knowledge of French.

As a visitor staying in the tourist resorts, you will get by without difficulty speaking English or French, but in informal situations, a few Creole expressions, such as *li bon* (that's good/fine) or *ki manière?* (how are you?) or *tout correk* (okay) are always appreciated. If you're in Mauritian company, you'll find that the conversation may take place in Creole, French or English or a combination of all three.

Mauritian women with temple offerings

FLORA AND FAUNA

More than three hundred years of human settlement have significantly altered the vegetation and wildlife of Mauritius. Little remains of the original flora, other than a few patches of forest, declared as nature reserves, in the centre of the island and on some offshore islands. The dodo's demise in the seventeenth century (see page 19) is only the most publicised extinction of the island's birdlife. Now only seven species of endemic birds remain, the most noted being the Mauritius kestrel, the pink pigeon and the echo parakeet. These birds can be seen in the Black River Gorges and the Bambous Mountains, while the pink pigeon is the star attraction on Île aux Aigrettes nature reserve off Mahébourg.

Imported fauna include deer, monkey, the tenrec (a tail-less hedgehog), mongoose and the wild boar. There are three species of gecko, several tree lizards and the *couleuvre*, a non-poisonous snake introduced from India. Wildlife is generally harmless,

The rare pink pigeon

although extra care should be taken to avoid stepping on stonefish, whose spines can inflict serious injury.

SUGAR, TOURISM AND BEYOND

Many fruits and vegetables and small amounts of coffee are grown for home consumption, although rice, a staple food, has to be imported in large quantities from Asia. Sugar cane is the dominant crop. Great tracts swathe the island, giving the land a fresh, green tropical appearance virtually year-round.

Once the island's most important industry, sugar production has given way to tourism and textile manufacturing, bringing Mauritius much-needed foreign income. However, increased competition coupled with a drop in demand and the global recession has resulted in the closure of many textile factories. Despite this setback, economic diversification has continued apace. Mauritius promotes itself as an offshore banking centre, and a scheme to transform Mauritius into a 'cyber island' has seen the construction of business premises now partly occupied by major foreign companies. Real estate development has accelerated with the introduction of the Integrated Resort Scheme (IRS), allowing high-worth non-residents to invest in luxury residences in Mauritius. The latest real estate development scheme is 'smart cities' – mixed real estate and retail/entertainment complexes – which have sprung up on land owned by sugar estates.

Despite being hard hit by the prolonged closure of its borders due to the Covid-19 pandemic, Mauritius is still a highly desirable tourism destination. It has become a 'green tourism' island, with inland activities – such as rock climbing, soft safaris, nature walks, canyoning and quad and mountain biking – now available on land owned by the sugar estates. Such excursions make a welcome change from the beach, revealing a multi-faceted island. It has also made steps towards sustainable agriculture, with much of the produce for hotels now sourced locally and a movement towards organic ('bio') food afoot. Meanwhile, luxury villas are springing up at top hotels and resorts, together with a surge in more affordable accommodation, making the island more than just a holiday dream.

The vibrant red of the flame tree

HISTORY AND CULTURE

Eight million years ago, Mauritius rose from the depths of the south-western Indian Ocean in a series of volcanic eruptions. Réunion and Rodrigues followed a couple of million years later. These three islands are today known as the Mascarenes, named after the Portuguese admiral Pedro Mascarenhas, who visited the area in 1513.

The volcanic activity carved out a distinctive landscape of mountains, craters and coastal plains; lagoons and reefs were later additions. Trees and other plant life gradually covered the Mascarenes, which became the exclusive preserve of millions of birds attracted to a sea teeming with marine life. Prominent bird species included the flightless dodo of Mauritius and the solitaire of Rodrigues. However, human occupation soon led to the extinction of these species and the decimation of indigenous forests.

EARLY SETTLERS

Early fifteenth-century Arab maps show Mauritius as Dina Arobi and Rodrigues as Dina Moraze, but there is no evidence that Arab explorers ever settled on either island. The first European visitors were the Portuguese in the early sixteenth century, who named Rodrigues after the navigator Diego Rodriguez, and christened Mauritius after his ship the Cirné, Ilha do Cirné. Later Portuguese explorers and traders used the islands as convenient bases on the long voyages between the Cape of Good Hope and India but, like the Arabs, they never settled. However, they did leave a lasting legacy by deliberately introducing cattle and monkeys so that there would be fresh meat supplies when ships called. These introduced animals, including rats and dogs escaping from ships, upset the delicate ecological balance that had existed for millions of years. In about 1539, the last Portuguese sailors left Mauritius and the island was unoccupied for more than fifty years, save for occasional visits by pirates who roamed the Indian Ocean.

THE ARRIVAL OF THE DUTCH

The Dutch arrived in 1598, landing in the southeast of Mauritius at Vieux Grand Port, a natural harbour near present-day Mahébourg, and named the island after Maurice (Maurits) of Nassau. They built a fort, the remains of which were excavated in 1997, and settled along the coast where they planted crops – including sugar cane – and began to cut down the ebony forests for export. With the French and British vying for this valuable commodity, the settlers realised that the harbour in the northwest was vulnerable to invasion and sent a small detachment of troops to what is the present capital, Port Louis. But cyclones, drought, food shortages and quarrels among settlers led to a Dutch withdrawal from the island in 1658.

In 1664 another attempt at colonisation was made when the Dutch East India Company, based in Batavia (present-day Jakarta, Indonesia), realised the strategic importance of Mauritius in the context of the sea route between Europe and the Indies. The new settlers cleared more ebony forests, introduced deer to overcome food shortages and imported enslaved people from

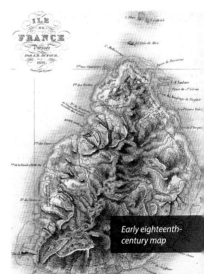

Early eighteenth-century map

The extinct dodo

Madagascar and convicts from southeast Asia to work the fields. But apathy, an inefficient administration and pirates' attacks forced them to leave the island for good in 1710. All that was left was a group of escaped enslaved people. The only humans who came ashore were crews of visiting ships and pirates (possibly from the fabled Malagasy pirate republic, Libertalia). The pirates targeted the expanding maritime trade route between Europe and the Indies, raiding the ships of the various East India companies.

FRENCH COLONISATION

The French arrived soon after the Dutch left; in 1715, they took possession of the island and renamed it Île de France. The first French colonists landed at Mahébourg in 1722, but dangerous reefs and contrary winds threatened their ships, so they moved to the safety of Port Louis. Piracy continued throughout the French period. The French issued letters of marque to pirates and owners of private ships, authorising them to attack foreign vessels in the name of France. The holders of these letters became known as corsairs or privateers.

In 1735 Bertrand François Mahé de La Bourdonnais, a naval officer, arrived at Port Louis as the new governor of the Mascarene Islands and set about transforming Île de France into a flourishing colony. A large labour force was crucial to his plans, and he began importing thousands of enslaved people from Africa and Madagascar. Ships were built, farms improved, roads constructed and forests cut down to make way for sugar plantations. With French supremacy now well established in the Indian Ocean, the French East India Company supplied ships and stores to Port Louis for campaigns against the British in India.

In 1767 the company suffered heavy financial losses following the defeat of the French by the British in India. La Bourdonnais was falsely accused of bribery and imprisoned; Île de France was handed over to the crown. The French Revolution of 1789 had

THE DEMISE OF THE DODO

Mauritius' best-known indigenous bird, the dodo, is the world's most famous example of extinction and a symbol of man's destructiveness. The bird was fat, friendly and flightless. Clumsy and tame to the point of foolishness, this 23kg (50lb) bird made easy prey for the first Dutch settlers in the early seventeenth century; they killed thousands of dodos for their meat. At the same time, the bird's eggs and chicks made tasty morsels for introduced animals, such as rats, monkeys and dogs. Some live dodos were taken to Europe and exhibited as the most fantastic living freaks of the day. By the late seventeenth century, however, there were no more dodos to show off – the species had become extinct.

Pont Etienne by Thuillier, 1847

little effect on the islanders; if anything, the influence of new ideas manifested itself in a wave of loose living. The elite, bound by their shared belief in slavery, had their own revolution in 1796 when France sent two officials to announce that slavery would be abolished. The colonists' fervour for liberty, equality and fraternity wore thin and the officials, amid rioting and unrest, were promptly sent back home.

Conflict with the British intensified, with the French using corsairs to attack British shipping. Between 1793 and 1802, corsairs captured more than a hundred East India ships, which were brought to Port Louis. The capital soon earned a reputation as a den of thieves where ruined adventurers and swindlers provided the corsairs with a ready outlet to dispose of stolen goods.

Île de France's period of autonomy lasted until 1803 when Napoleon appointed a new governor, General Decaen. Decaen curried favour with the elite by allowing slavery and privateering, both hugely profitable, to continue. Meanwhile, the British continued to lose valuable cargo to the corsairs.

BRITISH COLONISATION

After months of blockading Port Louis, the British based themselves on Rodrigues and took the island of Réunion before launching a major naval attack in 1810 on Mahébourg. The four-day Battle of Grand Port ended in defeat for the British, who lost four frigates. However, a few months later, in December, a vast British fleet landed at Cap Malheureux and troops marched to Port Louis. The French offered only token resistance and Île de France became a British colony, reverting to its former name, Mauritius.

The British capitulation terms were generous: anybody who wanted to leave could do so and was given free passage home, while settlers were allowed to keep their laws, customs, language, religion and property, a term which included enslaved people. By eliminating Mauritius as a corsair base and establishing a governor and garrison, the British achieved supremacy in the Indian Ocean. English became the official language, but the island retained much of its French character.

Under Robert Farquhar, the first British governor, Port Louis became a free port, roads were built and trade flourished. Sugar production soared and sparked an ever-rising demand for enslaved labourers to clear land and plant cane – even though slavery had been abolished in the British Empire in 1807. In 1832 Judge John Jeremie was appointed procureur-general and duly arrived in Mauritius to announce abolition without compensation to hostile planters and enslavers. He was forced to leave almost immediately. In response, the British built Fort Adelaide (La Citadelle) on a hill overlooking Port Louis to quell demonstrations. Slavery was finally abolished in 1835.

Britain turned to the Indian subcontinent for cheap labour to maintain sugar production. During the nineteenth century, nearly half a million Indians arrived at the Aapravasi Ghat in Port Louis

Grand victory

The 1810 Battle of Grand Port was the only French victory over the British at sea during the Napoleonic Wars. The battle's name is inscribed on the Arc de Triomphe in Paris.

and were set to work in the sugar plantations. Working conditions were not far short of slavery. They were paid a pittance, worked long hours and were often subjected to harsh treatment.

In 1872 a royal commission was appointed to look into the problems of Indian immigration. The Indians' living standards improved slightly and immigration was finally halted in 1909 when another royal commission recommended social and political reform. By now, many Indians had settled in Mauritius; today, their descendants comprise most of the population.

In 1936 the Indians took political action and campaigned for better working conditions. Strikes the following year and again in 1943 brought the sugar industry to a standstill. The British responded by drawing up plans for constitutional reform. But the real turning point came in 1959 when the first elections under universal suffrage were held and subsequently won by the Labour Party under a Hindu doctor, Seewoosagur Ramgoolam (who was later knighted).

INDEPENDENCE

In 1968 Britain agreed to grant independence on condition that the British take over the Chagos Archipelago, a group of islands 1,930km (1,200 miles) northeast of Mauritius. These islands, inhabited by the Chagossians (Îlois), had been part of the British colony of Mauritius since 1814 when France ceded them to Britain. In 1965, a secret deal was made between Britain and the United States whereby in exchange for leasing one of the islands in the group, Diego Garcia, for fifty years, the British Government would get a discount of $11 million on Polaris submarines. The islands were detached from Mauritius and became part of the new British Indian Ocean Territory (BIOT). The Chagossians were displaced and taken to Mauritius, where they were dumped at the docks and left to fend for themselves. Diego Garcia is now a major US military base, off limits to all. The long-held hope of Chagos islanders to return to their homeland remains a distant dream.

In the run-up to independence, fears arose that politics would become 'Indianised', and many Mauritians settled abroad. In 1968 Sir Seewoosagur Ramgoolam became the first prime minister.

In the early 1980s, following a series of corruption scandals, high unemployment and over-population problems, the opposition party, the Mouvement Militant Mauricien (MMM), swept into power. After that came several governments that were coalitions of the four major parties.

In 1992 Mauritius became an independent republic within the Commonwealth. The Queen was replaced as head of state by a locally nominated president.

MODERN MAURITIUS

Since independence, the island's dependence on sugar has lessened. Manufacturing and textile industries rose in importance beginning in

Indian labourers

A nation's father

The first prime minister of Mauritius, Sir Seewoosagur Ramgoolam (1900–85), became known as 'the Father of the Nation'. The Royal Botanic Gardens of Pamplemousses were renamed in his honour two years after his death.

the 1970s, but today the country's main markets for manufactured goods are turning to cheaper sources elsewhere. Many textile factories have closed and unemployment is around 7.4 percent.

While still a significant pillar of the economy, sugar production no longer employs the vast numbers it used to. Changes to international sugar pricing agreements have hit the industry hard, and sugar barons are turning their lands over to real-estate development and tourism.

Tourism remains the primary foreign income earner and, despite being hit hard by the Covid-19 pandemic, has bounced back stronger than before and with a stronger emphasis on sustainability. Luxurious golf and spa resorts, and eco-tourism attractions, such as La Vallée de Ferney and Bel Ombre Nature Reserve, are attempts by the industry to show visitors another facet of the island beyond the sea and beaches. And, in March 2022, the Mauritius Kestrel – a conservation success story – replaced the dodo as the official national bird.

'Paradise Island' may be for those who come for the magnificent beaches, but Mauritius is the most developed African country. Back in 2005, the country launched itself into information and communications technology with the opening of Ebène Cybercity, now Mauritius' main business hub, and 'smart cities' – mixed residential, retail and entertainment complexes - are springing up across the island. The expansion of Western-style residences attracts a new wave of expatriates, mainly from South Africa, who bring modern ideas from farmers' markets to pop-up eateries.

HISTORICAL LANDMARKS

1400s Arab names of Dina Arobi and Dina Moraze for Mauritius and Rodrigues appear on early maps.

1513 The Mascarene Islands are named after Portuguese navigator Pedro Mascarenhas.

1528 Diego Rodriguez, a Portuguese seaman, visits Rodrigues and gives the island his name.

1598 Dutch land at Port South East.

1638–1710 Dutch settlers attempt to colonise Mauritius; introduce sugar cane, Java deer and pigs. First enslaved people were imported from Madagascar.

1691–93 François Leguat and nine others settle Rodrigues.

1715 French annex Mauritius, naming it Île de France.

1721–1810 French traffic hundreds of thousands of enslaved people to the Mascarenes.

1735 La Bourdonnais becomes the first governor of the Mascarene Islands.

1793–1805 British East India Company suffers considerable financial losses due to privateering. French Revolution and Napoleonic Wars provoke revolutionary fervour in Mauritius.

1810 British seize Île de France, renaming it Mauritius.

1814 The Treaty of Paris places Mauritius, Rodrigues and the Seychelles under British ownership; Réunion is handed back to the French.

1835 Slavery Abolition Act (1833) comes into force; the British institute indentured labour.

1909 Indian immigration ceases. British Parliament appoints a royal commission to make recommendations for political and social reform.

1968 Mauritius becomes independent. Rodrigues becomes a dependency. Seewoosagur Ramgoolam is elected prime minister.

1992 Prime Minister Anerood Jugnauth proclaims Mauritius a republic.

2002 Government of Mauritius grants Rodrigues regional autonomy.

2017 Pravind Kumar Jugnauth becomes prime minister, winning another five-year term in 2019.

2018 Mauritius celebrates fifty years of independence from Britain.

2022 Mauritius lifts all Covid-19 entry requirements.

The colourful Central Market in Port Louis

OUT AND ABOUT

This guide divides Mauritius into bite-size geographical chunks. Port Louis, the capital, and the plateau towns are worth a visit at least once to experience contemporary island life. The north coast (the northwest in particular) is home to the most established resorts. The more isolated east coast may be too windy for some during winter, but the hotels here offer pure luxury and access to lovely offshore islands. The west coast, renowned for stunning sunsets, has fine diving and watersports and is within easy reach of the rugged Black River Gorges, as is the developing south coast. The small island of Rodrigues, a newcomer to tourism, offers a total contrast to Mauritius, with simple hotels, rugged landscapes and a predominantly Afro-Creole population.

PORT LOUIS

In 1735 Bertrand François Mahé de La Bourdonnais, the governor-general of the Mascarene Islands, founded this settlement on the northwest coast. With 150,000 residents crammed into less than 10 sq km (4 sq miles) and thousands of workers who arrive daily from nearby, it's no surprise that **Port Louis ❶**, like most capitals, is crowded, dirty and noisy. It lacks any real architectural wonders and makes no claim to urban chic. Still, its fascination lies in its jumble of Franco-British colonial buildings juxtaposed against modern office blocks and a hotchpotch of tumbledown shops dwarfed by modern mini-skyscrapers.

Surrounding the city are the picturesque peaks and knolls of the Moka Mountains, including the aptly named Le Pouce (*le pouce* means 'thumb' in French), the tapered pinnacle of Pieter Both, named after the Dutch admiral who drowned nearby, and

The Caudan Waterfront

the massive bulk of Signal Mountain to the south. It's an atmospheric city with statues and monuments shaded by palm trees, colourful Chinese and Indian temples and churches, and a bustling market and modern waterfront. The often debilitating summer humidity reminds you that you are in the tropics.

Every visitor should try to spend at least a morning exploring the back streets of Port Louis with its tiny 'hole in the wall' shops, bargaining in the market and eating on the hoof along with the lunchtime crowds. Apart from Le Caudan Waterfront (locally known as Le Caudan), it's not a city that stays awake after dark.

THE WATERFRONT

Built in 1996 to replace the old harbour, the pedestrianised **Le Caudan Waterfront** (Mon–Thurs 9.30am–7pm, Fri 9.30am–8pm, Sat 9.30–8.30pm, Sun 9.30am–2pm; free; tel: 230 211 9500, www. caudan.com) **Ⓐ** complex has become the focal point of the capital. Its two modern hotels, oceanarium, 24-hour casino, designer boutiques, restaurants, arts centre and businesses are housed in renovated coaster sheds and dockside buildings. Despite recent developments, the sights of the harbour remind you that this is a working port: the industrial landscape of docks and quays includes the squat, solid red-brick Granary building (now a car park), the spruced-up Bulk Sugar Terminal, as well as cargo ships.

In 1847 Mauritius became the fifth country in the world to issue postage stamps (see page 68); the very first stamps – the Mauritian Two Penny Blue and One Penny Orange-Red – are now extremely valuable. This philatelic history is displayed south of the waterfront in the **Blue Penny Museum** ❸ (Mon–Sat 10am–5pm; charge; tel: 230 210 9204, https://bluepenny.museum). The philately exhibits include examples of both stamps, and there are fine artworks, old maps, coins, postcards and historic photographs.

To the north, behind a smart arcade of souvenir shops, is the **Windmill Museum** (Mon–Fri 10am–noon, 1–3pm; free), a reconstruction of the original flour mill built by the French in the eighteenth century. Inside, a collection of old photographs of Port Louis shows the waterfront's transformation, plus anchors and cannon found during the renovation works. A children's play area provides a distraction for young families.

Also on the waterfront is the colonnaded **Post Office**, built by the British in 1868, and the **Postal Museum** (Mon–Fri 9.30am–4.15pm,

THE MAURITIAN FLAG

Port Louis is most colourful on Independence Day (12 March), when Government House and other public buildings are festooned with the national flag. The Mauritian flag consists of four horizontal coloured bands in red, blue, yellow and green. Officially red represents freedom and independence, blue the sea, yellow the lights of independence shining over the nation and green the swathes of sugar cane that are so characteristic of the country. Others maintain that the colours reflect the island's multi-faith community: red is for the followers of Hinduism, blue for the Catholic community, yellow for the Tamils and green for the Muslims. Mauritius celebrated fifty years of independence in 2018.

Indian influx

Within a decade of the first immigrants from India in 1834, half a million more arrived, making Mauritius the British Empire's biggest recipient of Indian labour and its most successful sugar-producing colony.

Sat until noon; charge; tel: 230 213 4812, www.mauritiuspost.mu/philately/postal-museum), which has a small collection of nineteenth-century telegraph and stamp-vending machines, postal stationery and printing plates. The museum is a good place to buy first-day covers and commemorative stamps.

Nearby are the gardens of the **Aapravasi Ghat** Ⓖ (Mon–Fri 9am–4pm; tel: 230 217 7770, https://aapravasi.govmu.org/aapravasi). This area was an immigration depot for the first indentured Indian labourers who arrived in 1834 to work on sugar estates in conditions not far removed from slavery.

In 2006 Aapravasi Ghat was given UNESCO World Heritage Site status; it is recognised as the place where the 'modern indentured labour diaspora' began. You can wander around the atmospheric basalt buildings and through a museum where scenes of immigrant life are depicted on bronze murals.

The latest attraction to open on the harbour is **Odysseo Oceanarium** Ⓓ, the Indian Ocean's largest (daily 9am–6pm; charge; tel: 230 659 8000, www.odysseomauritius.com) is worth visiting for its collection of reef and lagoon fish displayed in several huge tanks, feeding the rays and a shark encounter. It is situated adjacent to Le Suffren Hotel & Marina.

OLD PORT LOUIS

Place S Bissoondoyal (formerly **Place d'Armes**, and still called this by locals), directly opposite the waterfront, is a good place to start a tour of **Old Port Louis**. Here the statue of Mahé de La

Bourdonnais stares out to sea. Shaded by an avenue of royal palms and flanked by banks and offices, this one-way street is the heart of the capital and Port Louis' busiest thoroughfare. At the end of the street is **Government House** Ⓔ, built on the site of a tumbledown wooden shack later enlarged by La Bourdonnais as his headquarters when he transformed the city from an Indian Ocean backwater into a thriving seaport. A marble statue of Queen Victoria and, behind it, a statue of Sir William Stevenson, the British governor from 1857 to 1863, are reminders of the city's colonial past. To the right, on the corner of La Chaussée, are the former **Treasury Buildings** built in 1883, now the prime minister's office, with large overhanging verandas providing respite from tropical downpours.

Along La Chaussée is the **Natural History Museum** Ⓕ (Mon, Tues, Thurs & Fri 9am–4pm, Wed 11am–4pm, Sat 9am–noon, Sun & public holidays closed; free), an attractive cream-coloured colonial building fronted by a huge baobab tree. Beyond the museum are **Company Gardens**, where the French East India Company had its headquarters. Today, with its bottle palms, giant banyans and statues of famous island sons, it is a pleasant lunchtime setting for office workers.

The **Municipal Theatre** Ⓖ, built in 1822 on Intendance Street, is the oldest theatre in the Indian Ocean. Despite being closed for extensive

Government House, Port Louis

The city's racetrack

renovations, it remains a symbol of the city's culture.

Across the road from the theatre and tucked down the cobbled lane of Rue de Vieux Conseil is the **Museum of Photography** (Mon–Fri 10am–3pm; charge; tel: 230 211 1705). The building is crammed with impressive displays of late nineteenth-century photographic equipment, postcards and historical photographs of Port Louis.

City Hall and the adjacent government buildings are examples of the uninspiring concrete architecture of the 1960s. Still, you can't avoid them getting to the Roman Catholic **St Louis Cathedral** Ⓗ in Cathedral Square. This twin-towered neo-Gothic cathedral, dating from 1932, is the third to be built on this site, both of its predecessors having been destroyed in cyclones. In the chapel are the remains of Madame La Bourdonnais and her son. The fountain outside, with its four bronze lions, dates back to 1786 and provided water for city folk. Immediately behind the cathedral is the fine nineteenth-century colonnaded mansion of the **Episcopal Palace** with its high ceilings and wide verandas.

The cream-coloured Anglican **St James Cathedral**, hidden in tranquil Poudriere Street, occupies the site of a former gunpowder store where the French incarcerated British prisoners of war. The British built the single-spired cathedral in 1828 and installed a bell that once belonged to a French governor.

At the eastern edge of Port Louis and cradled by the Moka Mountains is the **Champs de Mars** racecourse, the oldest in the southern hemisphere, best seen from the heights of **La Citadelle** ❶ (Mon–Fri 8am–4pm; charge), a now abandoned basalt-built lookout post built to the north by the British in 1832. Under the French, the area was a military training ground and in 1812, it was turned into a racecourse by Colonel Edward Draper, a British army officer. Fringing the north side in Dr Eugene Laurent Street is a colourful Chinese temple bedecked with ornate scripts. For respite from the heat, make for the walking trails at **Le Dauget** in the foothills of the Moka Mountains; there are panoramic views of the city and harbour.

After 160 years of providing Port Louisiens with fresh produce from a dilapidated site between Queen and Farquhar streets, the **Central Market** ❷ relocated into an adjacent two-storey locally-built stone and timber building. All that remains of the old market are the Victorian wrought-iron gates and a meat and fish section. The new market (Mon–Sat 7am–3pm, Sun 7am–noon), which has its main entrance in Queen Street, is worth visiting for its bustling atmosphere, brash colours, strange smells and unexpected sights. You can barter for baskets, clothing, spices and even salt fish and honey, wend through the fruit and vegetable stalls or buy a herbal remedy 'guaranteed to cure all ills'. The ground floor is packed with fruit and vegetable sellers and there is an air-conditioned food section selling traditional Mauritian meals, snacks and drinks. The upper floor has a small eating area, more souvenir stalls, and great market views.

Perhaps the most eclectic part of the city is several

Built to survive

The walls of St James Anglican Cathedral were built 10ft (3m) thick to make them cyclone-proof, allowing Port Louisiens to shelter inside when these fierce tropical storms struck.

blocks east of the market towards the pagoda-like entrance of **Chinatown Ⓚ**. The air is thick with the smell of herbs and spices and the streets bristle with specialist food shops, Ayurvedic shops, small eateries and chaotic supermarkets. Standing sentinel on the corner of Jummah Mosque Street and Royal Road is the green and white **Jummah Mosque** (https://jummahmasjid.org). Built in 1853, it is the island's most impressive mosque, with ornate teak doors and decorative walls. You will need to ask permission to visit the courtyard.

Three Chinese temples, open to the public, are some distance from Chinatown. The oldest is the **Kwan Tee Pagoda**, beside the busy roundabout south of Le Caudan Waterfront, dedicated to the Chinese warrior god. Another, known as the **Chinese Pagoda**, is located on the corner of Generosity and Justice streets, where the scent of sandalwood drifts from the red and gold interior. There is a Buddhist shrine on the first floor affording fantastic city views. The most serene is the cream-coloured **Thien Thane** temple in the verdant foothills of Signal Mountain on the southeast edge of town. Remember to remove your shoes when entering a temple.

Also on the foothills of Signal Mountain and a world away from the brouhaha of town is the peaceful shrine of **Marie Reine de la Paix**. In 1989 this place of pilgrimage was crammed with thousands of islanders gathered to hear mass said by Pope John Paul II. The Catholic community still uses it for religious gatherings. From the wide paved walkway and lovely lawned terraces, there are great views of the city and harbour.

Line Barracks Ⓛ, which has its public entrance on Jemmapes Street, sits squarely around a central courtyard and takes up several city blocks. Built in 1764 by the last governor of the French East India Company to house troops who had previously been billeted in private homes, today it is the headquarters of the Mauritius Police Force. It is arguably one of Port Louis' quirkiest sites. Learner drivers take their licence test here, gingerly steering a course round gardens containing

The Thien Thane temple

a petrified dodo and the odd cannon or two and past the city prison dubbed 'Alcatraz' before emerging into the busy streets through an incongruous blue-tiled archway marked 'Gateway of Discipline'.

OUTSIDE PORT LOUIS

The **Church and Shrine of Père Laval**, to the northeast of Port Louis in the suburb of **Sainte-Croix**, is dedicated to the French missionary Jacques Désiré Laval, who arrived in 1841 to convert Black freed people to Catholicism. When Père Laval died in 1864, his special healing powers became legendary, and in 1979, the Catholic Church beatified him. The modern white church replaced the original, which was damaged by Cyclone Carol in 1962. It is worth visiting for its abstract-style **stained-glass windows**, lofty convex timber ceiling and modern mosaics depicting the life of Christ. Beside the church stands a vault containing a stone sarcophagus enclosing the remains of Père Laval's body beneath an effigy framed with flowers and candles placed by people of all faiths. There is also a small shop selling postcards, books and souvenirs of a religious bent, and plenty of information in French and English on the life of Père Laval. The adjacent **presbytery** is a superb example of nineteenth-century colonial architecture.

South of the capital at **Montagne Ory** is the colonial mansion called **Eureka – La Maison Creole** ❷ (Mon–Sat 9am–4.30pm; charge; tel: 230 433 8477/5727 4457, www.eureka-house.com). Built

Eureka

in 1856 by an Englishman, it was later auctioned to the wealthy Leclezio, a Franco-Mauritian family, one of whom cried 'Eureka' when his bid was accepted. This ancestral home is now a museum, although it could do with some TLC and a lick of paint. Built entirely of indigenous wood, the main house has 109 doors, and the high-ceilinged rooms are filled with antique furniture that reflects a bygone era. You can take tea or a traditional lunch on the spacious veranda of the main house, explore the external stone-built kitchen equipped with original Creole cookware or take a riverside nature walk through tropical gardens towards a deep ravine and waterfall.

THE NORTH

The coast north from Port Louis attracts the most visitors to Mauritius because of the stunning stretches of white, sandy beaches backed by turquoise lagoons, the fine hotels, and the popular resorts of Trou aux Biches, Grand Baie and Péreybère. The region also has access to a collection of offshore islands and several inland attractions, providing a distraction for beach lovers and watersports enthusiasts. Although hotels maintain the best beaches, no beach is private and as long as you don't access them via the hotel entrance, you are free to use them.

A fast dual-lane carriageway, locally referred to as the 'motorway', links the north to Port Louis, with a series of roundabouts leading to villages and on to the various resorts.

Inland, sugar cane clothes a flat landscape broken by the gentlest of hills. From July to December, when the cane is harvested, there are superb views to the south of Port Louis' Moka Mountains, which provide a natural compass from which to get your bearings if you're walking, cycling or driving. At other times of the year, the sugar cane is so high that the view is obscured and travelling is like being in a maze, although somebody is always around to ask for directions.

NORTH FROM PORT LOUIS

A series of sheltered bays and long stretches of beach pepper the coast north of the capital. First is **Le Goulet**, an attractive white crescent of sand nestling between low cliffs and backed by a forest of casuarinas just off the Arsenal road. Next is the **Baie du Tombeau** (Bay of the Tombs) on the B29. In 1615, four Dutch East India Company ships were caught in a cyclone, which swept them onto the reef here. Everybody drowned, including Admiral Pieter Both, after whom the Port Louis mountain peak is named.

The next bay is **Baie aux Tortues** (Turtle Bay), dominated by appealing beach hotels that flank the River Citron's banks. Here, ammunition was supplied for French expeditions to India from an arsenal at nearby Moulin a Poudre. The bay is a designated marine park popular with snorkellers, but nearby hotel developments have damaged the corals. At nearby Balaclava are some ruins of a nineteenth-century private estate and a waterfall on the grounds of the Maritim Hotel.

The small village of **Pointe aux Piments** hugs the shore, revealing glimpses of local life and a lovely rocky beach backed by grassy verges dotted with religious shrines. Inland, at Mapou, is **Château de Labourdonnais** (daily 9am–5pm; charge; tel: 230 266 9533/3007, https://domainedelabourdonnais.com), said to

Maheswarnath temple

be modelled on Versailles and reached through an attractive avenue of London plane trees. The grounds are as lovely as the house, with a gourmet restaurant overlooking the lawn, ancient fruit orchards and a rum distillery.

Trou aux Biches, a former fishing village, has developed into a popular international resort with a proliferation of shops, supermarkets and eateries. The 3km (2-mile) white, sandy beach includes a public beach, but much is dominated by the Trou aux Biches Beachcomber Hotel. At nearby **Triolet** is the island's largest Hindu shrine, built in 1857, the imposing **Maheswarnath Temple**. You may be asked for a donation in return for a guided tour, which you should place directly into the sealed box at the entrance.

The most popular public beach is further north at **Mon Choisy** ❸. Here, a grassy football pitch, a former landing strip, is marked with a monument commemorating the first flight from Mauritius to Réunion in 1933 by two French pilots, Hily and Surtel. At weekends the blindingly white beach is crammed with campers in makeshift tents and families feasting on *farathas* and curries; impromptu *sega* dances take place beneath the shade of a dense casuarina forest. Mid-week, it is an ideal location for snorkelling, swimming, strolling or horse riding. Don't miss the Hindu shrine on the beach near Mystik Lifestyle Boutique Hotel, one of the few spots to enjoy a drink by the sea. At the back of the beach, **Pointe**

aux Canonniers (Gunners Point), reached through an avenue of flamboyant (flame) trees from Mon Choisy, is a historic headland. The French used it as a garrison and shore battery and the British as a military and quarantine post. Today, this is a tranquil coastline indented with pristine beaches, and the only surviving colonial remains are a nineteenth-century lighthouse and a few cannons on the grounds of Canonniers Beachcomber Golf Resort & Spa.

GRAND BAIE

At the end of the motorway, the appeal of **Grand Baie ❹**, billed as The Mauritius Riviera, lies in the profusion of shops, restaurants and cafés not attached to hotels strung around a milky turquoise bay dotted with pleasure craft. Called overrated by some islanders, who point to its lack of pavements, congested coast road, tatty tourist shops and night-time sex work, Grand Baie, for most European holidaymakers, is heaven, thanks to its slow, easy-going atmosphere and range of hotels, apartments and self-catering accommodation mostly within walking distance of the action. In Chemin Vingt-Pieds, **La Croisette** (tel: 230 209 2000, www.gblc. ennovatek.com), a massive entertainment and leisure complex with eighty shops, twenty restaurants, cinemas and luxury apartments, sparked off retail and real estate development in the area.

The centre of operations is Sunset Boulevard, where designer shops rub shoulders with cafés, souvenir shops and the **Sportfisher Big Game Fishing Centre** (https://sportfisher.mu). Tour operators line the street, offering car and bicycle hire, excursions and trips to offshore islands and water-based activities, such as diving, water-skiing, windsurfing, parasailing, underwater safaris and undersea walks. For a swim, avoid the beach on the coast road and head to **La Cuvette** at the north of the bay, where the boho-chic beach club, **N'Joy** (tel: 230 5500 8601, https://njoy.mu), beckons. This cove has a parking area, showers, food kiosks and toilets, and you can swim beyond the basalt rocks on the right-hand side and onto the beach fronting the celebrity-starred Royal Palm Beachcomber Luxury hotel.

NORTH FROM GRAND BAIE

Just 2km (1 mile) north of Grand Baie is **Péreybère**. It offers affordable self-catering apartments, a fairly buzzing nightlife in bars and beach-fronted eateries, safe swimming and a handy bus route linking it with Port Louis. It is popular with independent travellers as an alternative to brash Grand Baie. At weekends, convoys of mobile food wagons, ice-cream vans and lorries crowded with picnicking families from Port Louis liven up this normally quiet beach.

Shallow bays and rocky coves combine to make a picturesque 6km (4-mile) journey north via Bain Boeuf to the island's

A tropical idyll at Grand Baie

most northerly point, **Cap Malheureux**. A pretty red-roofed church surrounded by grassy lawns overlooks the lagoon to the wedge-shaped island of Coin de Mire, directly opposite. In 1810 a massive British naval force anchored off its shores before marching to Port Louis to take possession of Mauritius.

More sparkling beaches backed by casuarina forests unfold at Anse la Raie before the road hits the cane fields leading to **Grand Gaube**, a fishing hamlet fanned by northeast trade winds. Beyond the gates of the area's two main hotels, LUX Grand Gaube and Veranda Paul et Virginie, lie a pleasant public beach, children's play area and coast road with colourful tumbledown village stores.

Filthy Corner

The area now known as Pointe aux Canonniers was dubbed by early Dutch settlers De Vuyle Hoek (Filthy Corner) because so many of their ships were swept onto the reef.

South of Grand Gaube is the bustling town of **Goodlands**, where a textiles and clothing market (Tues & Fri) attracts hundreds of locals and a few tourists. Directly opposite the market is the island's biggest maker of model ships, **Historic Marine** (Mon–Fri 8.30am–5pm, Sat–Sun 8.30am–noon; tel: 230 283 9404, www.historic-marine.com; free guided tour), where models based on original museum plans, and nautical furniture, are produced and sold. Tucked behind high walls near Winners supermarket is **La Demeure Saint Antoine** ❺ (Tues–Sat noon–3pm and 6–9.30pm; tel: 230 2821823, http://lademeuresaintantoine.com), a nineteenth-century mansion with a colonnaded veranda, and original works from famous Mauritian painter, Malcolm de Chazal. You can wander around the interior as part of a visit for lunch or dinner.

To the southeast of Goodlands is **Poudre d'Or**, where an obelisk on the headland opposite the reef commemorates the sinking of the *St Geran* in 1744 and the drowning of a young engaged couple. The event inspired eighteenth-century writer, Bernardin de Saint-Pierre, to pen the romantic Mauritian classic *Paul et Virginie*, after whom a hotel at Grand Gaube is named. Some of the wreckage from the *St Geran* is displayed at Mahébourg's National History Museum (see page 48). For a great day's snorkelling in translucent waters, local fishermen will ferry you to uninhabited **Île d'Ambre**, or you can take a kayak trip with **Yemaya Adventures** (https://yemayaadventures.com). For some bracing walks along windy, deserted rock-studded beaches, head further south to isolated **Roches Noires**, but do not swim here because the currents are dangerous. The adventurous may want to explore the underground network of lava tubes, which is open to the public but best visited with a guide.

NORTHERN OFFSHORE ISLANDS

Operators in Grand Baie offer full-day tours with barbecue lunch to all the offshore islands, including popular Île aux Cerfs (see page 45) in the east and Île aux Benitiers (see page 65) in the west. The reef-enclosed waters between Flat Island and Gabriel Island are most pristine for swimming and snorkelling. On Flat Island, pathways, a lighthouse and a cemetery bear testimony to those who died during the 1856 cholera epidemic, while the deserted beaches of Gabriel have changed little since the island's days as a quarantine post. Great coast views from the open sea and deep crystal-clear waters for snorkelling make a cruise to **Coin de Mire** a wonderful excursion, although going ashore here is not possible due to the island's crumbling volcanic rock. **Round Island** (which isn't round) is home to the rare Telfair's skink and **Serpent Island** (which has no snakes) is a bird sanctuary. Both are designated nature reserves closed to visitors.

PAMPLEMOUSSES AND THE SUGAR MUSEUM

The north's top attraction is the **Sir Seewoosagur Ramgoolam Botanic Garden** ⑥ (daily 8.30am–5.30pm; charge), commonly known by its former name, Pamplemousses Botanic Gardens, at **Pamplemousses**. Well signposted on the motorway north of Port Louis, the gardens are only a thirty-minute drive from Grand Baie. A visit makes a pleasant change from the coast. Official guides (charge) may offer to show you around the 25-hectare (62-acre) site, but you can wander the maze-like shady palm-lined avenues bordered by indigenous Mascarene island flora at will. Impressive sights include the graceful yellow and white lotus flowers of the Lotus Pond and the huge, flan-case-shaped leaves of the giant Amazon water lilies in the Lily Pond. Other specimens include the curiously named marmalade box, chewing gum and sausage trees. In 1735 under Governor Mahé de La Bourdonnais, the area was used as a market garden and provided fresh supplies for the ships calling at Port Louis.

Giant Amazon water lilies in the botanic gardens

Among the other notable sights here are the white wrought-iron gates, which were included as an exhibit at the Great Exhibition of 1851 at London's Crystal Palace. The imposing **Chateau de Mon Plaisir**, built in the mid-nineteenth century by the British, was named after the original chateau occupied by Pierre Poivre, the French intendant and horticulturist who first introduced many species that grow here today. Opposite the gardens is the eighteenth-century **Saint François d'Assise Church**, fringed by a handful of restaurants, cafés and souvenir shops.

L'Aventure du Sucre Museum (Mon–Sat 10am–4pm; charge; tel: 230 243 7900, www.aventuredusucre.com), just 0.5km (0.25-mile) from Pamplemousses at Beau Plan Sugar Estate, is a former sugar factory converted into a fascinating museum. You can easily spend half a day here exploring, with the aid of videos and interactive displays, the history of sugar and its importance to Mauritius's social and economic development. Original equipment includes huge mill wheels, evaporation tanks and an old sugar boat authentically anchored in a reconstructed indoor harbour. Guided tours are also available, as well as free sugar tastings. There is a shop selling speciality sugars and unusual souvenirs, plus the pleasant Fangourin restaurant and a behind-the-scenes tour of the Patrick Mavros atelier, which makes one-of-a-kind jewellery.

THE EAST

Although some of the island's most luxurious hotels are located on the east coast, this area remains essentially isolated and rural, an area of agricultural land broken by vistas of picturesque mountains,

Looking out over Coin de Mire

slow-moving fishing villages and inviting beaches. Many hotels lie in sheltered positions, protected from the southeast trade winds that blow year-round but are especially strong from May to November. Away from the beaches, some rewarding historic and scenic attractions can be explored. Getting around by public transport can be frustrating and it may be better to hire a car.

BELLE MARE TO ÎLE AUX CERFS

The main town is **Centre de Flacq**. Apart from the Wednesday and Sunday market, tumbledown shops and a nineteenth-century courthouse, there's little to see here but plenty of buses and taxis to other parts of the island. East of the town, through flat cane fields, is the beautiful **Belle Mare** ❼ public beach lapped by an idyllic lagoon. Barbecue areas, the odd mobile food wagon and meandering paths

through the casuarinas replace the straw parasols and swanky sophistication of the hotels flanking the beach, while old lime kilns testify to the former industry of coral burning.

South along the coast road, the small village of **Trou d'Eau Douce** has narrow streets, colourful tourist shops and simple restaurants. Nearby, a ten-minute boat service shuttles visitors from Pointe Maurice to **Île aux Cerfs** ❽ (www.ileauxcerfs leisureisland.com) every thirty minutes from 9.30 to 6pm. The island comprises 280 hectares (700 acres) of luxuriant woodland, an 18-hole golf course, three eateries and a few souvenir shops. You can wander along shaded paths, find deserted beaches, snorkel and swim, try a wide array of watersports, including parasailing, or stroll across to uninhabited Île Mangenie (there is a restaurant at the far end owned by Shangri La's Le Touessrok hotel, but you need to be a guest to eat there). If you want a Crusoe-style night on the island, book a bubble lodge or an eco-lodge by the beach or in the trees.

South of Beau Champ, sugar cane fields stretch towards the Bambous Mountains, which form a dramatic backdrop to the isolated fishing villages of Deux Frères, Quatre Soeurs and Grand Sable. The road hugs the shore until rising to **Pointe du Diable** (Devil's Point), a grassy headland, where Creole superstition credits the devil with upsetting the compasses of passing ships. Two cannons dating back to 1759 mark the site of a French battery, from whose ruined walls there are fine views of **Île aux Phares**. This was the island on which the Dutch imprisoned Rodrigues' first settler, François Leguat (see pages 72 and or click here), in 1693.

Vieux Grand Port, lying in the shadow of Lion Mountain, marks the beginning of a historic route along the coast. In 1598 the Dutch landed here, called it Warwyck Bay and built Fort Frederick Hendrik at the north of the town. It is now a collection of ruined walls with evidence of eighteenth-century French defences. The adjacent **Fort Frederick Hendrik Museum** (Mon, Tue, Thurs–Sat 9am–4pm, Wed 11am–4pm, Sun 9am–noon; free; tel: 230 634 4319, https://mauritiusmuseums.govmu.org) contains a model of the original fort, artefacts unearthed during a 1997 archaeological dig, and audiovisual displays of the history of the Dutch East India Company in Mauritius.

At **La Vallée de Ferney ❾**, to the west of Vieux Grand Port, you can take a guided nature walk or four-wheel drive tour from the visitors centre to the Ferney Conservation Park, with a guaranteed sighting of the Mauritius Kestrel (daily 9.30am–5pm; charge; tel: 230 660 1937, www.ferney.mu). This 200-hectare (500-acre) reserve contains endemic flora and fauna, viewpoints and offers DIY hiking trails for a nominal charge. If you like, you can stay at the exclusive Ferney Nature Lodge, nestled in the hills.

MAHÉBOURG TO BLUE BAY

Lying on the southern shores of the bay of Vieux Grand Port with views of Lion Mountain to the north is **Mahébourg** 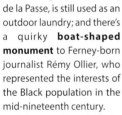, named after Mahé de La Bourdonnais. It is a laid-back village, which despite its bustling Monday market and dilapidated stores and shops, strives to maintain its colonial heritage: the streets, laid out in a grid pattern, are named after early European settlers; a waterfront promenade leads to an obelisk facing the pretty private islet of **Mouchoir Rouge** commemorates the Battle of Grand Port in 1810; an eighteenth-century washhouse called **Le Lavoir**, off Rue de la Passe, is still used as an outdoor laundry; and there's a quirky **boat-shaped monument** to Ferney-born journalist Rémy Ollier, who represented the interests of the Black population in the mid-nineteenth century.

A short stroll north of the village is **Cavendish Bridge**, which crosses La Chaux River to **Ville Noire**, named after enslaved Black people who arrived in appalling conditions to work the French-owned sugar plantations. Tucked around the back streets is the oldest

Mill wheels at L'Aventure du Sucre Museum

factory in Mauritius, the **Rault Biscuit Factory** (Mon–Fri 9–3pm; charge; tel: 230 631 9559, http://biscuitmanioc.com/home.html), where *biscuits manioc* are made from the cassava root. This family-run firm offers guided tours finishing with vanilla-flavoured tea and freshly baked biscuits. A scenic drive past the factory along the B7 through cane fields backed by the gorgeous Creole Mountains leads to **Riche en Eau**, where chimneys mark the site of early family-run sugar estates.

Mahébourg's **National History Museum** (Mon, Tues, Thurs, Fri 9am–4pm, Wed 11am–4pm, Sat–Sun & public holidays 9am–noon; free; tel: 230 631 9329, https://mauritiusmuseums.govmu.org) housed in a renovated colonial mansion on the A10 leading out of the village towards the airport, is worth a visit. Built in 1722 and the former residence of a French dignitary, it was hastily turned into a makeshift hospital in 1810, where injured commanders of the French and British fleets convalesced following the Battle of Grand Port (see page 21).

The museum contains maps and documents from the Dutch, French and British colonial periods, a frieze of the Grand Port Battle, portraits of maritime personalities, wooden palanquins used by enslaved people to transport their masters, and artefacts recovered from East India Company shipwrecks. The most prized exhibits are the bell from the doomed *St Geran*, sunk off the east coast in 1744, and La Bourdonnais' four-poster bed.

Southeast of Mahébourg is the nature reserve of **Île aux Aigrettes** ⓫ (Mon–Sat 9.30am, 10am, 10.30am, 1.30pm, 2pm, 2.30pm, Sun mornings only; charge; tel: 230 631 2396, www.mauritian-wildlife.org) – boats to the island launch from Pointe Jérôme, near Preskil Island Resort. The Mauritian Wildlife Foundation (MWF) created the reserve to protect native flora and fauna, so a trip here will appeal to the conservation-conscious rather than those wanting a water-based fun day out. Be advised that the island gets very hot (take a hat and water) and can accommodate only twenty visitors on tours led by knowledgeable MWF guides. You will see giant Aldabra tortoises, bands of the once-endangered pink pigeon, rare plants and paths bounded by bronze models of extinct fauna. During World War II, the island was used for military purposes, and rare birds and plants lifted to safety during the MV *Wakashio* oil spill in 2020 have now returned. The old generator room from that time has been renovated. It includes a rooftop platform, which affords sweeping views of a canopy of indigenous trees representing a microcosm of Mauritius's original coastal habitat – a shop and small museum display models and paintings of many extinct species.

Belle Mare beach

Back on the mainland via the high-walled seaside bungalows of Pointe d'Esny, the road ends at **Blue Bay** ⓬, where an idyllic beach backed by casuarina trees faces the private islet of Île des Deux Cocos (www.iledesdeuxcocos.com) which makes a great day trip. The area lies in a designated marine park, whose crystal-clear waters allow excellent snorkelling and diving.

THE SOUTH

The remote, wild south, with its undulating cane-clothed land-scapes, forests, waterfalls, rivers and mountains, has none of the bustle of the more popular tourist resorts of the north. Its appeal lies in its natural beauty and the feeling that you are returning in time. However, the west part of the south coast has transformed with the completion of smooth, wide roads that give access to hotels and inland attractions.

The southern beaches are narrower than elsewhere and rivers flowing from the uplands have prevented coral reefs from forming in many places. The last of Mauritius's indigenous forests is in the island's southwest corner. By contrast, the historic southeast is a flatter, sugar-producing region of small towns and villages linked by roads crossing streams and rivers.

Whether you drive yourself or join a guided tour, there are several ways of exploring the south: combining it with a trip to the Black River Gorges or Chamarel; from Bel Ombre in the west where several luxurious hotels herald the start of an easy route east along the south coast; or from Mahébourg in the southeast.

BLACK RIVER GORGES NATIONAL PARK

Enslaved people who escaped (or *marrons*) used to hide in the rugged mountains, gorges and forests that today make up the **Black River Gorges National Park ⓭**, an area of 6,575 hectares (16,250 acres) in the southwest. Elsewhere, little remains of the island's indigenous flora and fauna, but here you might spot all nine of the island's endemic birds – the Mauritius kestrel and the green echo parakeet were brought back from the brink of extinction – and bands of macaque monkeys.

Heading southwest to La Marie, continue past cool pine forests to the island's largest reservoir, **Mare aux Vacoas**. Continue for 7km (4 miles) to the crossroads called **Le Petrin**, in the centre of the park, where an information centre (tel: 2305471 1128) marks the entrance to the park. Here you can buy a map of the walking trails, picnic in the adjacent Le Petrin Native Garden or explore

the boardwalk leading over marshy heathland, where native flora and medicinal plants are being regenerated. You can book a bird-watching tour in the Black River Gorges/Petrin with the **Mauritian Wildlife Foundation** (tel: 230 5258 813, www.mauritius-wildlife. org). There is also access to the gorge from the coast, from Tamarin/Black River, if you want to have a gentle walk by the tree-lined river – and if you want something more challenging, guided hikes can take you up to the centre from there. MWF also offer reasonably-priced VIP tours, such as going to spot seabirds in the Northern Islands

A diversion 2km (1 mile) east of Le Petrin on the B88 takes you to the water-filled volcanic crater of **Grand Bassin**, watched over by a towering sculpture of the Hindu god Shiva and the goddess Durga. They're the island's tallest statues at 32m (108ft). Hindus call the lake Ganga Talao (meaning 'Ganges Lake') because they believe the waters are linked to the River Ganges in India.

Heading into the national park itself, drive south of Le Petrin via **Plaine Champagne**, an isolated plateau of privet choked with the invasive Chinese guava, whose fruit islanders gather for its vitamin C content in winter. On the way, keep an eye out for the *bois de pomme* and *bois de natte* trees, often draped with orchids, ferns and lichens, so characteristic of the island's upland forest. Further west are two viewpoints over the Black River Gorges. The first is **Alexandra Falls**, but the more spectacular views are from the **Black River Gorges Viewpoint**, 8km (5.5 miles) from Le Petrin, where the deep, dark gorges unfold. The peaks of Rempart Mountain and Corps de Garde form a backdrop in the northwest.

The road twists and turns steeply downhill to **Chamarel**, where coffee is grown on the slopes. This tiny village, with its church, village hall and simple restaurants, attracts tour groups heading to the **7 Coloured Earth Geopark ⑭** (daily 8am–5pm; charge; tel: 230 483 8298, www.chamarel7colouredearth.com). **Chamarel Waterfalls** (free), at the entrance, is the highest in Mauritius at 100m (328ft). Best seen after heavy rains, the falls tumble from the River St Denis in the Black River Mountains to form the River du Cap.

Festival lake

During the annual Maha Shivaratri festival at Grand Bassin, thousands of devotees make offerings to Lord Shiva and pray at the waterside Hindu temples. At other times of the year, the lake is a place of quiet contemplation broken only by birdsong and cheeky chattering monkeys.

Nearby are the 7 Coloured Earths, a unique landscape of multicoloured earth thought to have resulted from uneven cooling of molten rock. Facilities include a cafeteria, shop, viewing platforms and a tortoise pen.

While up the hill, Ebony Forest **Chamarel** (daily 9am–5pm; entry fee; tel: 230 460 3030, www.ebonyforest.com), a refuge for the island's native flora and fauna, offers nature hiking and guided bird-watching along a raised walkway in the endemic forest, tree-planting and a viewpoint overlooking Le Morne Mountain.

Although Chamarel is known for its natural attractions, the red-roofed **La Rhumerie De Chamarel** on Royal Road (Mon–Sat 9.30am–4.30pm; entry fee; tel: 230 483 4980, www.rhumeriedechamarel.com) is a popular stop. A guided

A Mauritius kestrel

tour shows the process from crushing the sugar cane to distillation from July to December and finishes with a tasting of high-altitude Chamarel Rums. The on-site gourmet restaurant, L'Alchemiste, serves dishes using produce from the estate.

A winding but picturesque route from the Coloured Earths to **Baie du Cap** on the south coast cuts through sugar-cane fields and thick plantations of banana and travellers palms. At Baie du Cap, turn left to join the B9 to Bel Ombre or right to reach Le Morne Peninsula.

BEL OMBRE TO SOUILLAC

The area of **Bel Ombre** is associated with philanthropist and planter Charles Telfair, who arrived in Mauritius from Ireland in 1816. He bought the Bel Ombre Sugar Factory and turned it into a 'model sugar estate' by treating his enslaved workforce humanely, upsetting the local slave-owning fraternity by doing so. The factory

Black River Gorges National Park

and banana plantations that once fringed the coast are now given over to tourism.

Sugar is still grown in the area and transported to nearby factories, but all that remains of Telfair's factory are the chimney and outbuildings.

Now occupying the site are Heritage Le Telfair Golf & Wellness Resort, an 18-hole golf course, and the elegant nineteenth-century **Château de Bel Ombre**, a former haven for visiting estate dignitaries that has been transformed into an upmarket restaurant overlooking landscaped gardens with a Presidential Suite upstairs. The **World of Seashells** (Mon–Sat 6am–2pm; Sun & public holidays 6am–1pm; tel: 230 623 7984) at Place du Moulin features a private collection from around the world.

Heritage Le Telfair, Heritage Awali Golf & Spa Resort and Heritage the Villas can arrange excursions into the nearby private **Bel Ombre Nature Reserve** (daily; tel: 230 260 5102; https://

belombre.com), where there are great walking trails and four-wheel drive, quad- and buggy-driving opportunities. Steep, winding tracks lead to **Frederica** for picnics and a swim beneath a small waterfall, where a ruined mill stands on the site of an old sugar factory. Further inland, **Val Riche Forest**, with its deer-hunting area and miradors, is home to many indigenous trees.

West of Bel Ombre is the small fishing village of **Baie du Cap**, followed by the magical deep inlet of the same name. Pretty Baie du Cap is home to the Maconde viewpoint, worth climbing for a great view of Le Morne Brabant, as well as a monument to Matthew Flinders and a range of street food sellers. Chug along the old concrete parapet across the bay, the Savanne Mountains forming a natural backdrop; this area is undergoing tourism development.

If you continue west along the coast road, you reach Mauritius's most famous landmark and a symbol of slavery, **Le Morne Brabant** ❶❺. Inscribed on UNESCO's World Heritage List and commemorated on the International Slave Route Monument at the foot of the mountain (https://lemorneheritage.org/slave-route.html), this forbidding mountain towering over the hammerhead-shaped peninsula, now fringed with beach hotels, marks the former hideout of many escaped enslaved people. When slavery was abolished in 1835, a posse was sent here to announce the news. Fearing they would be hunted down, the enslaved people flung themselves off the mountain rather than surrender.

East of Bel Ombre, the coast road speeds past cane fields, crossing bridges over the jungle-like banks of the **River Jacotet**. The river flows into **Baie de Jacotet** opposite Ilot Sancho, where British and French troops clashed in 1810. There are rumours of buried pirates' treasure here.

The smooth B9 coast road from **Pointe aux Roches** to Riambel provides access to the luxurious Shanti Maurice Resort & Spa and public beaches. An unusual stop on this coast is **The Vortex** at

Chamarel Waterfalls

Riambel (daily 9am–5pm; tel: 230 5736 9038, www. vortexriambel.com), said to be one of fourteen energy vortices in the world. It's a meditative spot, and you can lie in the circle of coloured cabanas to 'recharge your chakras'. You can also drive inland from Chamouny to **Bassin Blanc**, where a precarious parking area allows views into a waterfilled crater where the rare green echo parakeet and the Mauritius kestrel thrive in the surrounding forest. Further east, the sea off Pomponette is known for its treacherous currents, but there is safe swimming at SSR Public Beach just before the peaceful hamlet of Riambel. This area is earmarked for real estate development.

There's nothing to detain you at Surinam, but if you're passing, it's worth stopping at **Souillac ⑯**, 2km (1 mile) further east, to explore a handful of nearby attractions. In the nineteenth century, steamships laden with cane from nearby estates would shunt along the coast to Port Louis from the old port on the banks of the River Savanne, where a 200-year-old sugar warehouse has been converted into the Le Batelage restaurant. A fun way to visit Souillac is by **electric bike tour**. Contact Explore Nou Zil (https://explorenouzil.com) to take you on an exploration of the area from Place du Moulin, to take in the history and isolated bays.

Just 5km (3 miles) inland from the old port, a bumpy ride through cane fields leads past the chimney of an early nineteenth-century sugar factory and the colourful Mariamen Temple before reaching the 10m (33ft) high **Rochester Falls**. The waters spill over from the Savanne River and years of erosion have shaped the basalt rock into upright columns. After heavy rains, young islanders use this place as an outdoor pool, it's a bit isolated, so it's advisable to visit as part of a group.

Just opposite Souillac's bus station is **Telfair Gardens**, perched on the edge of a cliff and shaded by Indian almond trees and banyans. To the west is the **Marine Cemetery**, which contains some

COLONIAL HOMES

Saint Aubin is a fine example of a once-widespread style of colonial architecture. Traditionally constructed from wood, colonial houses were kept cool by spacious and airy verandas at the front and rear and by windows decorated with ornate wooden friezes or lambrequins. Wooden shutters could be closed during cyclone periods.

Unless maintained against the ravages of tropical conditions, wooden houses deteriorate very quickly, and sadly, many colonial houses have been allowed to fall into ruin. However, some superb privately-owned residences are hidden in the sugar estates and the back streets of Port Louis. The finest example is the 1859-built **Château de Labourdonnais** (daily 9am–5pm; charge; tel: 230 266 9533/3007, https://domainedelabourdonnais.com) at Mapou. Restored to its former glory in 2010, this residence contains original furniture and an ambience of yesteryear. You can dine in colonial splendour in the restaurant, with a bar offering a tasting of its award-winning rum, surrounded by magnificent lawned gardens, or stroll through the estate and tropical orchards. The souvenir shop sells estate-produced food and drink.

of the island's oldest tombs, including those of Mauritian historian Baron d'Unienville (1766–1831) and poet and writer Robert Edward Hart (1891–1954), who lived in the village.

A ten-minute stroll east of Telfair Gardens is the **Robert Edward Hart Museum** (Mon, Tues, Thurs–Fri 9am–4pm, Wed 11am–4pm, Sat 9am–noon; free; tel: 230 625 6101), Hart's former home. This prolific Franco-Irish poet wrote works in French and English from this charming coral-built bungalow, which he called **La Nef** (The Nave). The interior contains personal belongings, laid out much as he would have left them.

For views of a savagely wild coast from a grassy wind-swept headland, walk a few minutes east to **Gris Gris**, the most southerly point of Mauritius and a place rumoured to be associated with black magic. A fine cliff walk reveals ghostly silhouettes of black rocks bashed by ferocious seas, including La Roche qui Pleure (The Crying Rock), which bears an uncanny resemblance to Hart's profile.

On the A9, 5km (3 miles) northeast of Souillac, is the grand nineteenth-century colonial residence of **Saint Aubin** ⑰ (daily 9am–5pm; free; tel: 230 626 1819, www.saintaubinloisirs.com), set in spacious flower-bordered lawns dotted with trees and with an anthurium plantation. You can have an elegant lunch on the veranda (reservations essential) and experience agricultural rum-making with a tasting and vanilla production. Tea is grown in the highlands around Bois Chéri, 10km (6 miles) north. You can see how tea is processed and packaged at the **Bois Chéri Tea Museum and Factory** (daily 9am–5pm; charge; tel: 230 676 3089), with tastings (and an optional lunch, using local produce) at the attractive restaurant, in a hilltop chalet overlooking a lake. A guided Tea Route Tour, which can be booked through tour operators, starts at Domaine des Aubineaux, a former tea planter's residence at Curepipe, and is followed by a visit to the factory at Domaine de

Le Morne Brabant

Bois Chéri, tea tasting at a hilltop pavilion and lunch and rum tasting at Domaine de Saint Aubin.

At **Rivière des Anguilles**, also off the A9 and just after the river of the same name, is **La Vanille Nature Park** ⑱ (daily 9am–5pm; charge; tel: 230 626 2503, www.lavanille-naturepark.com). Allow a few hours to visit this nature reserve, and douse yourself with insect repellent before exploring the shaded walking trails. You'll see thousands of commercially farmed Nile crocodiles in secure enclosures, luminous green geckos, chameleons, insects and butterflies. You can interact with tortoises (at all stages of development), the Mauritian Flying Fox and lemurs. A shop sells crocodile products and the restaurant specialises in crocodile meat dishes. Further north is the **Britannia Sugar Factory**, surrounded by spacious lawns and pineapple plantations. Like many other factories in Mauritius, it is no longer engaged in sugar production.

There's not much of interest on the B8, which heads east towards the airport at Plaine Magnien, other than a diversion off-road to Le Souffleur, a blow hole in the cliff at L'Escalier midway along the coast. At one time, during high tide, powerful waves would send spouts of water into the air. After years of erosion, the spout these days is more of a cloud of spray, but you can have a nice walk along this stretch of wild coast.

THE WEST

The island's 50km (30-mile-) long west coast, rapidly rising in popularity among overseas visitors, is dominated by the mountains and forests of the Black River area and fringed by white beaches and turquoise lagoons. The climate is hotter and drier than other parts of Mauritius, and it is sheltered from the wind in winter. The seas off the Black River coast are a mecca for big-game fishermen, especially between September and March when warm waters attract giant marlin and tuna. Added to these attractions are fantastic sunsets,

JEWISH DETAINEES

In the grey-walled St Martin's Cemetery, 127 identical tombstones are a sobering reminder of World War II. British authorities refused 1,580 Eastern European Jewish refugees entry into Palestine in 1940. Regarded as 'illegal immigrants', they were shipped to Mauritius and detained in refugee camps at Beau Bassin Prison. They remained there until the end of the war. Families still return to Mauritius to visit the graves of those who died in the camps. You can find out more at the **Beau Bassin Jewish Detainees Memorial and Information Centre** (Wed–Fri 10am–4pm, Sun 10am–1pm; free; tel: 230 626 2503 https://jewishdetaineesmauritius.com).

great inland nature walks, fabulous dive spots and easy access to Port Louis.

SOUTH FROM PORT LOUIS

Just off the A3 south of Port Louis and almost mid-way down the west coast is the popular resort of **Flic en Flac**. There is a concentration of restaurants, shops, super-markets and Mediterranean-style apartment complexes, but the saving grace is the long white beach backed by

Le Gris Gris

casuarinas, a lagoon and distant views of Le Morne Brabant in the south. By contrast, **Wolmar**, less than 2km (1 mile) to the south, is quieter and dominated by half a dozen stylish beach-fronted hotels. The diving is excellent along the coast, with several wrecks to explore, including *Kei Sei 113* and *Tug 11*, sunk deliberately in the 1980s to form artificial reefs (see page 86).

The area north of the A3 cuts through the sugar-cane plantations of **Medine Sugar Estate**, which owns much of the land around Wolmar and the residential area of Albion. It is also one of the most successfully diversified estates on the west coast, with interests in tourism, golf resorts and real estate.

A few kilometres beyond the entrance to the sugar estate is the busy little village of **Bambous**. St Martin's Cemetery is tucked into cane fields to the north, where you can see the graves of Jewish detainees who died in captivity at nearby Beau Bassin Prison during World War II (see box).

Casela Nature Parks ⑲ (Mon–Sun 9am–5pm; charge; tel: 230 401 6500, https://caselaparks.com), on the A3 south from Bambous, makes a break from the beach and a fun day out. You could easily spend a whole day at the 10-hectare (25-acre) park, which sits on the flanks of Rempart Mountain. As well as some 1,500 birds, including the rare Mauritius kestrel and pink pigeon, housed in ninety aviaries, there are giant Aldabra tortoises, tigers, lemurs, antelopes and zebras. The top attraction is the chance to walk with lions and cheetahs in the wild, accompanied by their handlers, and interact with giraffes or a pair of adopted rhinos. Children can pet farm animals, and there's a reasonable restaurant with rolling views of the cane-clothed countryside. The more adventurous can join photo safaris, go quad and mountain biking or trekking, do some via ferrata or zip lining, or join exciting nature escapades in the adjacent Yemen Estate, where Java deer roam in a savannah landscape reminiscent of Africa. You are likely to spot wild boar, giant fruit bats and mongoose.

TAMARIN

Tamarin ⑳, 6km (4 miles) south, famous for its salt-making industry, is named after the tamarind trees introduced by the Dutch, a feature of the area, especially in the undulating terrain of the Tamarina Golf Estate. Luxury villas and an 18-hole golf course make Tamarin a fashionable place to holiday. The stylish Riverland Mauritius (tel: 230 483 4956), a sports and leisure complex with a large pool and cafeteria, attracts a

Martello towers

Martello towers were defensive forts built by the British in various coastal locations in Britain and the empire during the Napoleonic Wars. Their round shape and thick walls gave them great resistance to cannon fire.

trendy crowd; the Veranda Tamarin Hotel & Spa stages regular local live music nights, and the bay attracts dolphins and body surfers (in season), and offers kayaking trips. Meanwhile, the cosmopolitan village, favoured by expatriates, is growing fast, with developments like Cap Tamarin. The salt pans are now closed to be replaced by private villas, which are creeping up Tourelle Mountain and fringing a tranquil bay where the coral reef is subdued by waters flowing from the Rempart and Tamarin rivers in the central highlands. At sunset, there are magnificent views of Rempart Mountain from the bay, resembling a mini-Matterhorn in a tropical setting.

The **Martello Tower Museum** (Tues 9.30am–1pm, Wed & Sat 9.30am–5pm; charge; tel: 230 5471 0178, https://martello-tower-museum.business.site), at **La Preneuse**, sits on the northern side of the Grande Rivière Noire Bay, 2km (1 mile) south of Tamarin. It is the best-preserved Martello tower in Mauritius and has 3.5m

(11ft) thick walls. A visit takes you past cannon and the paraphernalia needed to fire them, including cannon balls; you'll see the fascinating engineering of the tower, how rain was collected in underground reservoirs and how gunpowder was kept dry. The British built this and four other towers on the large bays of the west coast to protect against enemy invasion at a time when there was much rivalry between the French-speaking population and the British authorities over the intended emancipation of enslaved people. Two other towers survive – at La Harmonie, south of the Grande Rivière Noire Bay, and Pointe aux Sables, just outside Port Louis.

Still on the A3 south, the next village, **Grande Rivière Noire**, is the west coast's game-fishing centre. Off the coast and beyond the reef, the seabed drops abruptly to a depth of nearly 600m (2,000ft), the habitat of several big-game species. Just before the village, opposite the Pavillon de Jade Chinese restaurant, a road cuts through sugar cane for 5km (3 miles) to the northern entrance of the Black River Gorges National Park. You can only drive as far as the visitors centre (daily 9am–5pm), where you can collect maps and information. Serious hikers may enjoy an uphill 10km (6-mile) trek along the strenuous Macchabée Trail, crossing rivers and streams to a spectacular

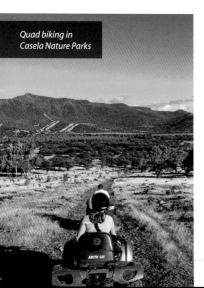

Quad biking in Casela Nature Parks

forest viewpoint. The other way to get into the park by car is to drive south to **Grande Case Noyale** and turn inland to Chamarel.

Grande Rivière Noire village sits on the estuary of a river that flows through some of the most rugged areas on the island. Once the poorest region of Mauritius, with a predominantly Afro-Creole population, the area is showing signs of prosperity, although life still trundles on at a leisurely pace. A gated complex of hillside villas and the somewhat-old-fashioned shopping and restaurant complex of Ruisseau Creole contrast sharply with the brightly painted stores, simple eateries and weathered timber-built colonial **post office** and **police station** of the village further on. Next to the post office is the **cemetery**, where the founder of the Mauritius Turf Club, Colonel Edward Draper, is buried.

At Grande Case Noyale, the cream-coloured church of Mater Dolorosa lies at the foot of a steep road marking the turn-off for the 5km (3-mile) drive to Chamarel. The road was initially built in 1812 to give access to the remote uplands, and although it is well surfaced and renovated in 2022, there are numerous hairpin bends. Spectacular views of the west coast unfold as you climb the timbered foothills of the Black River Mountains, and you may spot bands of macaque monkeys on the way. La Chamarel Restaurant and Varangue-sur-Morne, perched in the hills, provide panoramic views of the countryside, coast and clam-shaped **Île aux Benitiers** nestling in the lagoon. Both establishments are popular pit stops before pressing on to the 7 Coloured Earth Geopark.

THE PLATEAU TOWNS

The towns of the plateau have merged into one unattractive urban sprawl to form the district of Plaine Wilhems in the island's centre. Some 30 percent of the island's population live in this busy and often traffic-choked region. Despite these negatives, the towns are worth visiting for an insight into local lifestyles, the climate is cooler than elsewhere and there are isolated pockets of architectural interest.

The towns were formed a little more than a hundred years ago due to several migrations from Port Louis after fire, disease and cyclones sent inhabitants scurrying to the healthier uplands. Today the area of Plaine Wilhems contains the towns of Rose Hill–Beau Bassin, Quatre Bornes, Vacoas–Phoenix and Curepipe.

Many tour operators offer shopping trips to the towns, often combining them with a drive into the Black River Gorges. Still, you can just as easily drive yourself by taking the marked exits along the motorways linking Mahébourg in the south with Grand Baie in the north.

ROSE HILL–BEAU BASSIN

The Royal Road links the towns of **Rose Hill** and **Beau Bassin**, which are effectively one, with a combined population of about 150,000. Rose Hill's centrepiece is the Victorian-built **post office**, a former railway station, standing proud amid the chaos of the bus station fringed by ubiquitous food stalls and shopping arcades. The town shows signs of modernity, with new roads leading east past weather-beaten buildings to the Cybercity complex at Ebène. Here, **Cyber Towers 1 and 2**, occupied by foreign companies, are symbols of twenty-first-century development and reflect the island's desire to become a leader of information technology in the Indian Ocean region.

Meanwhile, **Arab Town**, in Royal Road, Rose Hill's main shopping street, is a reminder of the immediate present. Here, you can barter for just about anything under the sun among an untidy collection of corrugated-iron-covered stalls. Nearby, tumbledown shops are packed with incongruous displays of everything from statues of Hindu gods and the Virgin Mary to cosmetics and car parts. Further south is the colonial-style **Town Hall**, dating back to 1927 and a fine example of Creole architecture, and the Max Boullé Art Gallery, which sometimes exhibits works by local artists.

Île aux Benitiers

To the north along the Royal Road, **Beau Bassin** is less frenetic than Rose Hill and has a few sights worth visiting. **Balfour Gardens** (daily 5am–8pm) in Swami Sivananda Street has excellent views of the Moka Mountains across a ravine to a waterfall, which tumbles into the Grande Rivière North West. Next door is **Le Thabor**, a Catholic church pastoral centre. Charles Darwin stayed here in 1836, leading him to remark, 'How pleasant it would be to pass one's life in such quiet abodes'. More ravine views unfold in this tranquil area, dubbed 'The English Quarter' during colonial times when British diplomats and the aristocracy lived here.

At **Moka**, about 4km (2 miles) east of Rose Hill, is the modern university complex, the massive shopping Mall of Mauritius at Bagatelle and **Le Réduit**, the president's official residence (twice a year; check with the tourist office for dates). The French built this magnificent chateau in 1748 on a peninsula isolated by two ravines as a country residence and retreat for the wives and children of the French East India Company in the event of an invasion. It later became the residence of the British governor.

Nearby, the Mahatma Gandhi Institute has the **Folk Museum of Indian Immigration** (Mon–Fri 9am–3.30pm; free; www.mgirti. ac.mu), which traces the nineteenth-century migration of Indian cane workers to Mauritius.

QUATRE BORNES

Many people speed through **Quatre Bornes** after a shopping trip to La City, the European-style shopping mall at **Trianon**, unaware that some lovely colonial houses are tucked away in the back streets. La Foire market (Wed & Sat) in the heart of town has good buys in clothing, household goods, fruit and vegetables. The main Grand Route St Jean also has reasonably priced shops and eateries. To the west is the distinctive **Corps de Garde Mountain** at 720m (2,326ft), which escaped enslaved people used as a lookout post. Climbing the mountain's flanks are Hindu temples where

INVITATION TO A BALL

Le Réduit was the setting for a piece of philatelic history in 1847. That year, the Mauritian colonial authorities introduced postage stamps, one with a value of one penny and the other of two pennies. Britain had issued the first stamp only seven years before. The story goes that a local engraver was told to produce the stamps quickly so that the governor's wife, Lady Gomm, could use some of them to send invitations to a ball at the residence. The stamps, bearing the head of Queen Victoria, were mistakenly printed with 'Post Office' instead of 'Post Paid'. The mistake has made the few surviving examples highly valued by collectors. They are on display at The Blue Penny Museum in Port Louis.

Tamil devotees celebrate the annual Cavadee Festival (in either late Jan or early Feb). To the south is the hump-shaped **Candos Hill**.

VACOAS–PHOENIX

Vacoas was a former British land-based communications base, HMS *Mauritius*, whose old colonial-style buildings are now the headquarters of the paramilitary Special Mobile Force. The chaos of the bus station and market, so characteristic of many

Rose Hill church

Mauritian towns, is mitigated by more tranquil scenes: glimpses of rural England, with quiet, shaded avenues, an 18-hole golf course at the private Mauritius Gymkhana Club (www.mgc.mu), the oldest course in the Southern Hemisphere (tourists can play on a visitors' package), and the stone-built **St Columba's Church**, where services are held monthly in English.

Phoenix is home to a brewery producing local beer, food-manufacturing companies and the sprawling Jumbo and Les Halles shopping complexes.

Nearby, the **Mauritius Glass Gallery** (Mon–Fri 8am–5pm, Sat 8am–noon; free; tel: 230 696 3360) includes a small museum featuring exhibits by various conservation groups, such as the Mauritian Wildlife Foundation and Friends of the Environment. In the workshop, you can watch highly-skilled glass-blowers who use recycled glass and buy unusual products in the adjacent showroom.

CUREPIPE

Curepipe ㉑, the highest plateau town at 550m (1,840ft), is halfway between Mahébourg and Port Louis. In the eighteenth century, soldiers and travellers would rest and 'cure' or clean their pipes, hence the name. It was the first plateau town to be settled, mainly by the Franco-Mauritian population in the 1860s, who spilled into the suburbs of Floreal and Forest Side, where their descendants still live in grand colonial houses hidden by high bamboo hedges.

Invariably cloud-capped and rainy, the town is not particularly inspiring, but a shopping expedition can turn up the occasional good buy: porcelain and silk in the Chinese shops in Royal Road; designer goods, home decor and fashion accessories in the **Currimjee Arcades**, also in Royal Road; and antiques and art at **S'mall & Chic** at the corner of Sauzier et Sir Virgile Naz streets.

Moka mountain peaks

However, Tamarin and Grand Baie have strengthened their retail offering in recent years, and are probably a better bet overall for shopping.

Nearby, on Sir John Pope Hennessy Street, is the privately-run **Bobato Ship Models** shop (tel: 230 675 2899, https://bobatoship models.com; Mon–Fri 9am–4pm, Sat 9am–1pm). It's worth visiting for its collection of over a hundred model boats. The museum's owner is passionate about sailing history and is happy to share his knowledge with visitors. East of here, Curepipe's most attractive buildings are sandwiched between Elizabeth II Avenue and Ste-Thérèse Street near the market, whose concrete chimneys rise like foghorns against an often grey sky. Here the 1920s-built **Carnegie Library** and the impressive Creole-style architecture of the beautifully-restored **Town Hall** contrast with the modern Lake Point complex, with its casino. The Curepipe is also a popular gateway to the Black River Gorges National Park. A fifteen-minute walk or short taxi ride (vehicular access between 8am and 4pm) from the town centre is **Trou aux Cerfs**, a dormant volcano covered in a dense forest of vegetation. This 300m

Botanical Gardens

To the west of Curepipe are the 2-hectare (5-acre) Botanical Gardens on Botanical Gardens Street. Its avenues, bounded by lakes, lawns and indigenous plants, are perfect for a quiet stroll. Also worth a visit is **Domaine des Aubineaux** (tel: 230 676 3089, www.saint aubinloisirs.com), an attractive nineteenth-century colonial house in Forest Side. It's located at the start of 'The Tea Route'. Have a cuppa on the veranda overlooking exotic tropical gardens before heading to the Bois Chéri tea plantation for a tasting and lunch at Le Saint Aubin in the south.

(980ft) diameter crater was formed due to volcanic activity millions of years ago and is now choked with silt and water. At 650m (2,100ft) above sea level, you could be on the roof of paradise were it not for the urban sprawl of the plateau towns below, but the views of the mountains, especially on a clear day, are truly spectacular.

RODRIGUES

The island of Rodrigues, an autonomous region of Mauritius since 2002, lies 560km (350 miles) east of Mauritius. Shaped like a fish, it is 18km (11 miles) long and 8km (5 miles) wide, making it the smallest of the Mascarene trio. Only a few navigable channels penetrate the fringing coral reef, which protects a lagoon almost twice the island's size. Running the length of Rodrigues is a hilly ridge, from which a series of steep valleys drop to a narrow coastline. Even though the flight from Mauritius takes only an hour and thirty minutes, you can't help feeling quarantined from the rest of the world when you bump along the runway at Sir Gaëtan Duval Airport at Plaine Corail in the south. If you have lots of time (and the stomach for it), you can go to Rodrigues by ship, but this is not recommended (see page 123).

About 42,000 people live here. The island's distinct Creole-African atmosphere is in complete contrast to Indian-dominated Mauritius. Also, unlike Mauritius, the island is a relative newcomer to tourism. With stunning coves and bays, deserted beaches, a shallow islet-dotted lagoon, great diving, snorkelling, hilly walking trails, duty-free shopping, and a friendly, courteous people,

FRANÇOIS LEGUAT

François Leguat, who led the first group of settlers on Rodrigues in 1691, left behind a fascinating record of his time there, *Voyages and Adventures*. In it, he describes the island's unique flora and fauna, including a species of giant tortoise weighing over 135kg (300lb). There were so many tortoises that the beaches were covered in them, and Leguat used the shells as stepping stones to reach the sea (the species later became extinct). The book was so accurate that nineteenth-century naturalists and geologists used it as an early textbook. Leguat's name would have been forgotten had it not been for Rodrigues' star attraction being named after him (see page 80).

Rodrigues makes a simple, unpretentious and at times quirky holiday destination.

PORT MATHURIN

Port Mathurin ㉒, the pint-sized capital, is home to some six thousand people. It sits snugly on the north coast and was probably named after a French settler, Mathurin Morlaix, who arrived in 1726. Under the French, enslaved people from Mozambique and Madagascar, and settlers from Mauritius, increased the population to just over a hundred in 1804. Nobody took much notice of Rodrigues until the British launched an attack from its shores before taking Mauritius in 1810. They restructured Port Mathurin and laid out the present town in a grid style, naming many streets after surveyors and civil servants. Rodrigues's regional authority has now renamed the British-influenced street names with those of a French flavour.

A good place to start your exploration is from the boat-shaped jetty on the waterfront, where a **memorial** stands for volunteers who fought in World Wars I and II.

The Saturday **market** in Wolphart Harmensen Street attracts early risers as islanders set up fruit and vegetable stalls at 6am. You can find souvenirs such as baskets, wallets made from woven vacoas leaves, bottles of chillies, home-made chutneys, and fruit and vegetables. The market sells out quickly; by 10am, everybody has packed up and gone home.

The main artery of the town is Rue de la Solidarité one block back from the waterfront, where shops, no more than corrugated iron shacks with handwritten nameplates nailed to the door, contrast with a rash of duty-free shops in Rue François Leguat and Rue Morrison. In Rue Max Lucchesi, you can find unusual handicrafts, such as snazzy briefcases, straw hats and fiery home-bottled chillies. At the western end of Rue de la Solidarité is the tiny, white six-minareted **Noor-ud-Deen Mosque**. The island's only mosque was built in 1912 for the first Muslim settlers, who had arrived in 1907 as textile merchants.

Still in Rue de la Solidarité, hidden by white walls and fronted by a cannon, is the last vestige of British colonialism, the 1873 **Island Secretary's Residence**. It now houses the Rodrigues tourist office (Mon–Fri 9am–4.30pm; tel: 230 832 0866, www.tourismrodrigues.mu). The wide veranda is shaded by an Indian almond tree beneath which visiting colonial experts would discuss the next big move in island affairs.

A short stroll east leads to the Anglican **St Barnabas Church**, shaded by gardens and trees. Originally designed by an Eastern Telegraph cable man in 1903 as a shingle-roofed wooden chapel, it's been modernised and enlarged to encompass Rodrigues College. Most Rodriguans are Catholics and the little **Saint Coeur de Marie Church** in Ricard Street sees a regular Sunday congregation. The daubing of foreheads with ashes in the sign of the cross on Ash Wednesday, and processions on Easter Day, are serious traditions.

Across the **Winston Churchill Bridge**, which crosses the River Cascade, is the site of the first settlement on the island, in 1691, by French Huguenots fleeing religious persecution.

Led by François Leguat (see page 72), they lived for the next two years on 'very wholesome and luxurious foods which never caused the least sickness', as Leguat wrote, and feasted on fruit and palm wine, before returning to Mauritius only to be imprisoned by the Dutch on Île aux Phares as spies.

Further upriver towards **Fond La Digue** is Port Mathurin's only hotel, the delightful Creole-style Escale Vacances, set in a wooded valley overlooking the river. You can have some adventurous uphill walks along a jungle-like boulder-strewn track to Mont Lubin,

Returning to shore on Rodrigues

School visit

At Camp du Roi, next to the Care-Co Workshop, is the Gonzague Pierre-Louis Special Learning Centre (Mon–Fri 8am–2pm), a school for sight-impaired and hard-of-hearing children. Pupils are pleased to receive visitors and the teachers are happy to give you a tour.

where the Rodrigues fruit bat feeds on jamrosa trees at dusk.

For some unique island handicrafts, visit the **Care-Co Workshop** (Mon–Fri 8.30am–3pm, Sat 8.30am–noon; tel: 230 831 1766, www.careco-rodrigues.com) at Camp du Roi at the back of town. It is a charity where people with disabilities make coconut crafts and jewellery items. An apiary also produces the clear and distinctly flavoured Rodriguan honey, which has consistently won international awards.

Visitors wanting some nightlife, meanwhile, should look out for hand-written bills advertising *une grande soiree dansante*. These are big nights out, not to be missed, when you can let your hair down. On paydays and holidays or roughly once a month, everyone from babes in arms to robust Rodriguan grannies dance to seggae and reggae beneath flashing lights, surrounded by smooching couples. Try the alfresco discos at Les Cocotiers at Camp du Roi or the Recif at Anse aux Anglais.

AROUND PORT MATHURIN

A short stroll to the east of Port Mathurin is **Anse aux Anglais** ㉓ (English Bay), where, in 1761, a British fleet arrived and stayed for six months. Like the French ships before them, the Royal Navy's vessels transported thousands of giant tortoises – valued for their meat – from here to neighbouring Réunion. By the end of the eighteenth century, the Rodrigues tortoise, which may have numbered around two hundred thousand, had become extinct.

In 1901 cable men from the Eastern Telegraph Company (later Cable & Wireless) laid a submarine telegraph cable linking the island with Mauritius, thus completing the line of communication between Australia and Europe. The cable men lived in quarters at nearby **Pointe Venus**. The manager's colonial-style residence, which later saw service as the island's first hotel, reopened as a comfortable four-star billet but has now closed. There are good views across Port Mathurin from the headland where astronomers recorded the Transit of Venus in 1761, 1874 and 2004.

At low tide, near the old Pointe Venus Hotel, groups of fisherwomen, known as *piqueuses ourites*, make their living spearing octopus, which they hang out to dry in the sun. A stiff uphill climb from Anse aux Anglais via the tranquil beachside bungalows of **Caverne Provert** leads to a headland where there are resplendent views over sandy-bottomed **Grand Baie**, just 4km (2 miles) east of Port Mathurin. It's a lovely spot with only a church and a makeshift football pitch. From Grand Baie, the road peters out to become a narrow uphill track that leads towards the sweeping deserted beach at **Baladirou**. A less strenuous way of getting there is to take a forty-minute boat ride along the coast from Port Mathurin.

Just 2km (1 mile) west of Port Mathurin is **Baie aux Huitres** (Oyster Bay), an enormous bay surrounded

View over Port Mathurin

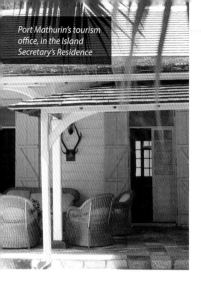
Port Mathurin's tourism office, in the Island Secretary's Residence

by hills and deep forests of casuarinas. Many civil servants posted from Mauritius live here with their families, alongside the predominantly European descendants of the first French settlers. For the best views, drive up to **Allée Tamarin**, a hamlet at the back of the bay.

INLAND FROM PORT MATHURIN

The bus station west of Port Mathurin has plenty of buses to take you on a bone-shaking journey around fearsome hairpin bends to the island's spine, where little villages overlook the north and south lagoons. Buses stop around 4pm, so leave plenty of time to return.

At **Pointe Canon**, there are panoramic views of the capital. On this windswept headland, you'll find a British cannon juxtaposed with a white statue of the Virgin Mary, **La Reine de Rodrigues**. On 1 May, the approach road and hills are a riot of colour, with islanders trekking towards the statue to celebrate Labour Day. On 15 August, many people attend outdoor mass here to celebrate Assumption Day. The road climbs to **Solitude**, where a forest bounded by deep valleys and eucalyptus trees is the habitat of colonies of fruit bats.

Mont Lubin, a busy little village of tumbledown shops, gives the impression of being at the top of the island, but the highest point is **Mont Limon** at 398m (1,289ft), a five-minute walk east. Many tourists pass this way to visit **Grande Montagne Nature Reserve** (Mon–Sat tours 9.30am & 1.15pm; charge; tel: 230 831 4862) for its walking trails and small museum before continuing to Pointe Coton and the isolated eastern beaches.

Rodrigues' biggest place of worship, the twin-towered Gothic-style Cathedral of Sacré-Coeur, is west along the Mont Lubin road at **Saint Gabriel** ㉔. Islanders built the cathedral in 1939, using donkeys to carry sand from the coast and their own labour to bring cement, lime, blocks of coral, corrugated iron and timber up the narrow mountain paths. It seats two thousand people and Sunday morning mass is a colourful event.

The 5km (3-mile) stretch of road between the hamlets of **Petit Gabriel**, **Quatre Vents** and **Mangues** is peppered with glimpses of translucent blue lagoons bordered by a thin pencil-line of ivory-white foam marking the reef.

You must pass through **La Ferme**, a large, noisy village where Pope John Paul II held a mass during his 1989 visit, to reach **Cascade Pistache**, 2km (1 mile) west of the village. This crater, hewn out of granite, is surrounded by grassy hills; the waterfall tumbling into Rivière Pistache looks particularly beautiful after heavy rains. As an alternative, take the road northwards to **Baie du Nord** for a scenic 9km (5-mile) coastal drive back to Port Mathurin, passing isolated homesteads swathed in poinsettias and hibiscus and causeways filled with mangroves at **Baie Malgache**.

THE SOUTH

From Mont Lubin, in the island's centre, it is only a 6km (3.7-mile) journey to **Port Sud-Est**. The road snakes its way down hillsides, twisting and turning along a series of hairpin bends, each giving glorious vistas of Port Sud-Est, where small coral atolls dot the lagoon. Your journey's end is **PLAY Mourouk Hotel**, picturesquely sited on an isolated clifftop. The nearest village to here is **Songes**, where boxy cyclone-proof houses are scattered along the hillsides. Attractions include leisurely walks to the pretty beach of **Petit Gravier** along the coast and picnicking and snorkelling excursions to Hermitage and Cat islands.

A visit to the coral caves with their fascinating stalactites and stalagmites at **Caverne Patate ㉕** in the island's southwest corner, some 18m (60ft) below the ground, is not for the faint-hearted. In 1786 bones believed to be those of the dodo were found, but later searches in 1894 proved that they belonged to a relative of the dodo, the solitaire, the bird described by François Leguat in 1691.

Safer, well-lit caves along timber walkways and handrails can be explored with qualified guides at the **François Leguat Reserve Rodrigues ㉖** (daily 9am–5pm; charge; tel: 230 8328 141, www. francoisleguatreserve.com) at nearby **Anse Quitor**. Here a conservation programme to restore the island's natural habitat is paying off with the planting of thousands of endemic plants and a colony

ÎLE AUX COCOS

For a day that will stay in your memory long after the holiday snaps have been stashed away, don't miss Île aux Cocos, 4km (2 miles) west of Rodrigues. Here you'll have nothing to do but pad barefoot along floury white beaches beside a gin-clear lagoon while listening to the chatter of birds. This island, one of eighteen inside Rodrigues lagoon, was transformed into a nature reserve in 1980 after studies revealed that only two were left out of an estimated twelve species of indigenous birds. It is now the last refuge of the fody and the brush warbler. Tour operators will arrange the necessary permits for a visit. The boat ride to Île aux Cocos ends 1km (0.6-mile) from shore because of shallow water; you walk the rest of the way.

of over three thousand introduced Aldabra giant tortoises at various stages of development. Allow half a day for a guided walk, including the island's only museum devoted to history, flora and fauna.

THE EAST

The **Cotton Bay Resort & Spa**, at Pointe Coton in the east, was the first three-star hotel to open in Rodrigues and is popular with walkers and beach lovers. Flanked by a low coral cliff, it overlooks

Cascade Pistache

the best swimming beach on the island. From here, you can walk to **Roche Bon Dieu**, a phallus-shaped rock symbol protruding from the earth and said to be a gift from God. There are more superb beaches, accessed by pathways on coral-topped cliffs, to **Anse Ally** – and Tekoma Boutik Hotel, the island's finest – **Saint François**, **Baie de l'Est** and to the protected forest land at **Tasman**. Due east from here, the nearest landfall is the western coast of Australia, some 5,500km (3,410 miles) away.

The forested area is fenced off to stop cattle grazing, but the watchman will let you in to experience some beautiful walks. Paths bounded by great forests of casuarina trees and acacias lead to a plateau of dead coral, where massive white rollers pound the reef, in some places less than 100m (300ft) from the shore. From here, the paths rise and dip into the lovely coves and bays of **Grand Anse**, **Trou d'Argent** and **Anse Bouteille** before linking up to Port Sud-Est.

Paddleboarding in warm waters

THINGS TO DO

SPORTS

Mauritius's greatest attraction is, of course, the sea. The coastal waters, with few exceptions, offer safe swimming in shallow blue lagoons. Most hotels offer free water-based activities, including snorkelling, windsurfing, water-skiing, Hobie Cat sailing, stand-up paddleboarding and trips in glass-bottom boats. Scuba diving, big-game fishing, kitesurfing and parasailing are also popular and can be booked through hotels or independent tour operators. Similar facilities are available in Rodrigues, but since that island's lagoon is shallow, there are no motorised watersports or parasailing. Big-game fishing is relatively new but spectacular.

The seabed and coral reefs are the habitat of myriad colourful fish and other marine creatures. Several operators offer enticing excursions, such as dolphin-watching cruises, underwater safaris, offshore islands cruises, tandem sky-diving and helicopter tours, which give magnificent views of the lagoons and coastline.

Recent years have seen a proliferation of green tourism ventures, for which reservations are essential. The undulating landscapes are ideal for horse riding, quad biking, buggy driving, four-wheel drive 'soft' safaris, mountain biking, cycling (pedal power and electric) and canyoning. Golfing on scenic courses, tennis (and increasingly padel tennis), walking and hiking are also very popular.

WATER ACTIVITIES

Big-game fishing. Mauritius holds the world record for giant marlin and hosts the annual Marlin World Cup competition in November at the Centre de Pêche, Grand Rivière Noire, in the southwest. The best time for big-game fishing is between October and the end of March or April when the waters beyond the reef teem with mighty blue and black marlin, yellow-fin tuna, wahoo, sailfish, bonito and various shark species. The larger hotels have boats and several private companies offer fishing excursions, such as the **Corsaire Club** (tel: 230 5835 5035, http://mauritius-big-game-fishing.com), **JP Charters** (tel: 230 5729 0901, https://jph.mu) and **Sportfisher** (tel: 230 263 8358, https://sportfisher.mu) at Grand Baie. A one-day fishing trip for a maximum of four people is about R40,000 and includes drinks in a fully equipped boat with an experienced crew. In Rodrigues, contact **Rod Fishing Club** (tel: 230 5875 0616, www.rodfishingclub.com).

Sailing. Cruising in catamarans, yachting or zipping by speedboat along the coast is immensely popular. Many charter companies offer full- or half-day excursions that include lunch, drinks and

Coral reef laces the seabed

snorkelling equipment. One of the best is **Croisieres Australes** (tel: 230 202 6660, www.croisieres-australes. com) at Moka, which offers an exhilarating day out from Grand Baie to Gabriel Island. **Totof** (tel: 230 5836 9065, www.totof-mauritius.com) at Blue Bay organises speedboat trips to Île aux Cerfs and the southeast islands. Tamarin-based **Lokal Adventure** (tel: 230 5934 8828, https://lokala dventure.com) offers a trip to four southeast islands by pirogue with a fish barbecue.

In Rodrigues, you can sail to several deserted islands within the lagoon through **360 Tours** (tel: 230 5811 6211).

Scuba diving. Dozens of dive centres, all affiliated with CMAS (World Underwater Federation), PADI (Professional Association of Diving Instructors) and BSAC (British Sub Aqua Club), are attached to hotels and offer courses for beginners and more experienced divers. All adhere to strict international safety regulations and provide multilingual instructors and all the necessary equipment.

Beginners start in the hotel pool before taking the plunge into the lagoon. Veteran divers should head for one of the long-estab-lished dive centres based around the island, such as Sun Divers at La Pirogue Resort & Spa, Villas Caroline at Flic en Flac, which offers specialist and night diving, and the independent Blue Water Diving Center in Trou aux Biches.

Sail away

For a Robinson Crusoe-style adventure, take a Catamaran cruise from Grand Baie to pristine Île Plate (Flat Island), which you can book through your hotel or direct through **Fanchette Group** (tel: 230263 5413/230 5766 2740, https://fanchettegroup.com). This exclusive trip includes a set menu lunch at Governors House – a nineteenth-century colonial ruin only steps from the beach, where *paille en queue* soar overhead – and a snorkelling session.

Some of the best dive sites are off the west coast at Flic en Flac, where there are several wrecks to explore, including the *Kei Sei 113* and *Tug 11*, sunk deliberately in the 1980s to form artificial reefs and now home to giant moray eels and myriad reef fish. Popular dives in the north include the wreck of *The Silver Star*, from 1992, and between two offshore islands, Gabriel and Flat. In the east, the prevailing winds limit diving opportunities, but some interesting dives can be made in and around the passes through the reef. The best place to dive on the south coast is at the Blue Bay Marine Park, where a sheltered lagoon and several sites beyond the reef will reward you with spectacular views of underwater life. On Rodrigues, there are dive centres at the **Cotton Bay Resort & Spa** (tel: 230 831 8001, www.cottonbayresortandspa.com) and **PLAY Mourouk Hotel** (tel: 230 832 3351, www.playmourouk.com).

Snorkelling. Many visitors are content to spend their entire holiday snorkelling in the safety of the lagoon and over the shallow reefs. If you're staying in a hotel, all equipment is provided; if you're not, there's no shortage of shops selling masks, fins and goggles. You can also buy waterproof laminated cards from bookshops identifying forty common reef fish species. Even if spending a short time snorkelling, do wear a T-shirt or rash vest and douse yourself in high-factor sun cream to avoid sunburn.

Submarine safaris. For a forty-minute trip in a submarine that enables you to have eyeball-to-eyeball contact with many marine species and explores an interesting shipwreck, contact **Blue Safari Submarine** (tel: 230 265 7272, https://blue-safari.com) or book through tour operators in Grand Baie. For a different kind of underwater adventure, you can drive on a sub-scooter 3m (10ft) under while breathing fresh air through a transparent dome surrounded by tropical fish.

Undersea walks. A boat takes you from the shore to a platform inside the lagoon. Wearing your swimsuit, you are equipped

Clear blue waters at Île aux Cerfs

with a helmet, which supplies fresh air piped from the surface by oil-free compressors. You are then gently lowered from the platform to the seabed, where you can stroll amid wonderful coral gardens and feed the fish by hand. The helmet allows verbal communication with an experienced diver who gives you a guided lagoon tour. This activity is safe for children over 7 years old and will also appeal to non-swimmers. Undersea walks can be booked through **Solar Undersea Walk Mauritius** (tel: 230 5253 6961, http://underseawalk.mu) at Grand Baie or **Aquaventure** (tel: 230 5729 3335, https://aquaventure.io) at Belle Mare.

Sea-kayaking. Family-friendly sea-kayaking trips around Île d'Ambre are offered by experienced operator **Yemaya Adventures** (tel: 230 5254 3205, https://yemayaadventures.com) while **Lokal Adventure** (tel: 230 5934 8828, https://lokaladventure.com) offers kayaking and dolphin-watching in Tamarin Bay.

Ready for rock climbing

LAND-BASED ACTIVITIES

Adventure Tourism. Mauritius is deemed the 'Adventure capital of the Indian Ocean'. Extreme sports enthusiasts can go canyoning and rock climbing with **Vertical World** (tel: 230 697 5430, www.verticalworldltd.com) or **Lokal Adventure** (tel: 230 5934 8828, https://lokaladventure.com). **Casela Nature Parks** (tel: 230 452 2828, https://caselaparks.com) offers quad biking, zip lining and a canyon swing, as well as safaris and interactions with African animals. For trekking and trail running, contact: **Yanature** (tel: 230 5251 4050, www.trekking-mauritius.com); or for trail walking and mountain biking, **Yemaya Adventures** (tel: 230 5254 3205, https://yemayaadventures.com). Local tour operators like **Mautourco** (tel: 230 604 3000, https://mautourco.com) have several adventurous options, such as mountain hiking, quad biking and kayaking, as well as an adventure trail into the hinterland to see hidden landscapes and visit traditional villages. In the **Black River Gorges National Park**, starting from Le Petrin or the Black River Visitors Centre (tel: 230 5914 9637) in the lower gorges, there are some 60km (37 miles) of easy-to-strenuous walking trails through tropical native forests. When choosing an operator for an adventurous activity, consider our health and medical-care information (see page 125), and check your travel insurance to make sure you're covered in case of an accident.

Horse riding. Several stables take visitors on rides through breath-taking hills and countryside, including **La Vieille Cheminee** (tel: 230 483 4249/5251 3551, https://lavieillecheminee.com) at Chamarel; **Haras du Morne** (tel: 230 5705 1644, www.harasdumorne.com) offers rides on the stunning foothills of Le Morne and 'swimming with horses' for experienced riders. Maritim Resort & Spa, on the northwest coast, also has private stables with ex-racehorses for guests' use. Reservations for horse riding are essential.

Cycling. The flat coastal regions make for some easy rides. Bikes and, increasingly, electric bikes can be booked through your hotel, and plenty of operators in the resorts rent bikes by the hour, half-day or full-day. Independent operator **Yemaya Adventures** (tel: 230 5254 3205, www.yemayaadventures.com) can deliver mountain bikes to your door, island-wide, if you want to hire one for longer. There are DIY mountain bike trails around the island, including 2km (1.2 miles) of off-road mountain trails in **La Vallée de Ferney** (tel: 230 660 1937, www.ferney.mu), which you can use for a small fee. **DunienZil** (tel: 230 5828 8685, https://explorenouzil.com) has fat and mountain bikes for hire and offers the best electric bike tours island-wide, including Chamarel, Grand Port and Pamplemousses.

Golf. With ten Championship 18-hole golf courses, Mauritius offers the best golf experience of any long-haul island nation. There are 9-hole courses at **One&Only Le Saint Géran** (tel: 230 401 1688, www.oneandonlyresorts.com), **Shandrani Beachcomber Resort & Spa** (tel: 230 603 4100, www.beachcomber-hotels.com/en), **Maritim Resort & Spa** (tel: 230 204 1000, www.maritim.com/en) and **Heritage Golf Club** (tel: 230623 5600, https://heritagegolfclub.mu). There are ten 18-hole courses on the island, including at **Anahita Golf & Spa Resort** (tel: 230 402 2200, www.anahita.mu/en), **Constance Belle Mare Plage** (tel: 230 402 2600, www.constancehotels.com/en), **Tamarina Golf Estate** (tel: 230 401

3006, https://tamarinagolfclub.com), **Paradis Beachcomber Golf Resort & Spa** (tel: 230 401 5050, www.beachcomber-hotels.com/en), **Heritage Golf Club** (tel: 230 623 5600, https://heritagegolfclub.mu) at **Île aux Cerfs Golf Club** (tel: 230 402 7720, www.ileauxcerfsgolfclub.com) on the east coast and at **Grand Baie Golf Club** (tel: 230 5252 8252, https://grandbaiegolfclub.com) in the north. Equipment, clubs and caddies can be hired. All hotels have a clubhouse with a locker room and shop. Pros can also be hired for lessons. Non-guests have to pay an entry charge. There is also a private 18-hole course at the **Mauritius Gymkhana Club** (tel: 230 660 1844, www.mgc.mu) at Vacoas.

OTHER ACTIVITIES

Horse racing. The season begins in May and culminates in November with the Maiden Cup, the year's grandest and most important race. Races are held every Saturday afternoon and some Sundays at Champs de Mars in Port Louis; taking a box at the races is a memorable experience. For further information, contact the **Mauritius Turf Club** (tel: 230 212 2212, www.facebook.com/MauritiusTurfClub2023).

Helicopter tours. Air Mauritius helicopters (tel: 230 603 3754, www.airmauritius.com/mauritius-helicopter-ltd) offer sightseeing tours and splendid photographic opportunities of the coast and interior. Prices vary depending on flying time and route. A fifteen-minute trip costs R20,000 for two (R4,000 per additional person), and helicopters can seat four people. A scenic flight in a modern H120 (Colibri) with **Corail Helicopters** (tel: 230 261 2266, https://corailhelico-mu.com/en) is priced at R5,000 for a ten-minute 'Heli-Sunset' for two.

Spas. The large hotels have luxurious spas with wellness and beauty packages, including everything from reiki and reflexology to hot stone massage, yoga and shiatsu. However, even three-star hotels in Mauritius usually have spas. Self-catering villas, and often guesthouses/B&Bs, can usually arrange spa treatments and yoga classes. Try the **Surya Ayurvedic Spa Centre** (tel: 230 263 1637) at Pereybere for dedicated Ayurvedic treatment at an independent spa.

Skydiving. For the jump of a lifetime, go tandem skydiving with **Skydive Mauritius** (tel: 230 5499 5551, www.skydivemauritius. com). Experience spectacular countryside and seascapes from 3,048m (10,000ft).

Food tours. Port Louis is known as one of the world's street food capitals, and the best way to find the best outlets is on a morning street food tour on foot. 'A Taste of History' with **My Moris** (tel: 230 5775 5516, https://mymoris.mu) weaves in history with every bite. **Taste Buddies** (tel: 230 266 7496, https://tastebuddies.mu)

An idyllic place for golf

The sega, a traditional dance imported by African slaves

explore the authenticity and diversity of Mauritian cuisine in Port Louis, Mahébourg and Grand Baie.

Cultural tours. Local tour operators typically offer visits to local craftspeople and Mauritian cooking sessions and lunch in islanders' homes. Tours from cultural specialists, **My Moris** (tel: 230 5775 5516, https://mymoris.mu), range from 'A Divine Morning', with a visit to a Hindu temple and a mouthwatering Mauritian meal to a Le Morne Mountain hike with an anthropologist, to learn about slavery on the island.

NIGHTLIFE AND ENTERTAINMENT

Most nightlife in Mauritius takes place in the hotels, which stage themed-after-dinner shows often featuring the _sega_, a traditional dance imported by enslaved Africans. Sexy and sensual, it is performed by voluptuous hip-wiggling women and accompanied by musicians beating wildly on the *ravan* (a goatskin tambour), the *maravan* (a hollow tube filled with dried seeds) and the triangle. Rodriguans have their own form of *sega* and traditional music, which you can see at hotels and during the five-day Festival Kreol, which takes place at the beginning of December. It can also be seen at the week-long Kreol International Festival in Mauritius in November/early December.

Away from the resorts, the nightlife is low-key, apart from several bars and discotheques in Grand Baie, Flic en Flac and Tamarin. Cultural activities are usually poorly advertised, so pinpointing what's happening can be tricky. Shows and musicals, invariably

TYING THE KNOT IN PARADISE

Couples seeking the perfect location for their wedding are finding it in increasing numbers among Mauritius's romantic seascapes and luxury hotels. But before vows can be exchanged, there are some legal necessities to attend to.

To get married in Mauritius, a couple must have a minimum of 24 hours' residency for civil ceremonies and fifteen days' residency for religious ceremonies. They must have a valid ten-year passport and bring original birth certificates, decree absolute if divorced, and, if getting married within ten months of the divorce, proof that the bride is not pregnant. Those aged under 18 must have parental consent. Legal proof of the change must be provided if names have been changed by deed poll. Once in Mauritius, the couple attends the registrar's office to sign an affidavit that they are both free to marry. For further information, contact the Registrar of Civil Status, 7th floor, Emmanuel Anquetil Building, Port Louis, tel: 230 201 3203. UK tour operators specialising in weddings are **Turquoise Holidays** (www.turquoiseholidays.co.uk) and **Kuoni** (www.kuoni.co.uk).

Model ships

Model ships of interest to collectors may be purchased from **Bobato Ship Models** (tel: 230 675 2899; https://bobatoshipmodels. com) at Curepipe and **Historic Marine** (tel: 230 283 9404; www.historic-marine. com) at Goodlands.

in French or Creole, are often performed at Mahatma Gandhi Institute at Moka and the Institut Français de Maurice at Rose Hill. **Casinos of Mauritius** (tel: 230 602 1300, www.casinosof mauritius.com) manage four casinos at Curepipe, Domaine les Pailles, The Caudan and Grand Baie. **The Senator Club** (tel: 230 413 8240, www. casinomauritius.mu) also has casinos island-wide, including at Port Louis, Triolet, Grand Baie, Mahébourg and Flacq. All the island's cinemas screen English-language films dubbed into French. For listings, visit https://cinema.mu.

SHOPPING

Local handicrafts include embroidery, paintings, basketry, model ships, pottery, recycled glassware and toiletries made from locally produced essential oils. Since the closure of many textile factories and increased competition from Asia, jewellery, knitwear, linen and textiles are not the bargains they once were. Several tour operators organise shopping trips to Port Louis, Floreal and Curepipe; alternatively, you can take a taxi and do it yourself. Shops to look out for are **Adamas** (tel: 230 686 5246, www.adamasltd.com), **Patrick Mavros** (tel: 230 260 4333, https://uk.patrickmavros.com) and **Cledor** (tel: 230 698 8959) for diamond and precious stones set in fabulous designs; **Passion** (tel: 230 5772 1241) for duty-free local and artisanal products, cashmere and linen goods. See www.taxfreeshopping.mu for duty-free shops island-wide. Beachwear and designer clothing under the Harris Wilson, Karl Kaiser, Marina Rinaldi and Max Mara labels are also excellent value.

Shops tend to have fixed prices, but you can test your bargaining skills in markets, of which there are dozens throughout the island. The most popular is the **Central Market** at Port Louis, renowned for its fresh fruit and vegetables and dozens of stalls selling clothing, spices and souvenirs; the large covered market at Flacq in the east; and the rustic traditional Monday market at Mahébourg. **Le Caudan Waterfront** in Port Louis, the **Mall of Mauritius** at Bagatelle and **La Croisette** at Grand Baie has changed retail therapy habits with vast shopping, leisure and entertainment complexes attracting upmarket customers from the more established outlets at Terre Rouge, Phoenix, Grand Baie, Floreal, Tamarin and the characterful arcades and tailor shops at Curepipe.

Supermarkets like **Jumbo** and **Super U** and the delightful **La Corbeille** delicatessen at **Domaine de Labourdonnais** (tel: 230 266 3004, https://domaine delabourdonnais.com) sell local produce at local prices. Look for attractive packages containing vanilla-flavoured tea, Chamarel coffee, confectionery, speciality sugars and spices. Gourmet rum, liqueurs and island-grown fruit-flavoured jellies also

Hand-carved sailing ship model

make good souvenirs, along with luggage-friendly vacuum packs of smoked marlin.

In Rodrigues, mind-blowing bottled chillies and pickles, delicious honey and a range of handicrafts made from coconut and other natural materials make unusual souvenirs. They can be bought from **Careco** (tel: 230 831 1766, www.careco-rodrigues. com) and other small outlets in Port Mathurin.

CHILDREN'S MAURITIUS

Mauritius is a very child-friendly destination with many safe bathing beaches and professionally run mini-clubs in larger hotels.

Animals are always a good bet when the appeal of splashing in seawater and building sandcastles starts to wear thin. The islands leading animal park, **Casela Nature Parks** (tel: 230 452 2828, https:// caselaparks.com), has an aviary and interactions with giraffe, rhino and tiger cubs, while crocodiles and tortoises are star attractions at **La Vanille Nature Park** (tel: 230 626 2503, www.lavanille-naturepark. com). For the very young, try the children's play area on Le Caudan Waterfront in Port Louis or the interactive displays at **L'Aventure du Sucre Museum** (tel: 230 243 7900, www.aventuredusucre. com) at Beau Plan.

Older children with a sense of adventure may like to go quad biking, zip lining and, providing they meet height restrictions, go walkabouts with lions and cheetahs at **Casela Nature Parks** (tel: 230 452 5546, https://caselaparks. com).

Takeaway flowers

Grown on a large scale in Mauritius, anthuriums, with their showy heart-shaped spathes and protruding flower spikes, make distinctive souvenirs or gifts. They are best bought in specially packaged boxes at the airport when you leave.

CALENDAR OF EVENTS

Many festivals are moveable dates and information on the more unusual events, such as fire- and sword-walking, celebrated by the Tamil community, is hard to come by. For more specific information about dates, times and venues of those shown below, contact the tourist office.

January/February *Cavadee* A Tamil festival in which devotees pierce their bodies and faces with skewers as penance to the deity Muruga. *Chinese Spring Festival* Celebration of the Chinese New Year with firecrackers and displays of dragon dances; the Chinese community offers gifts wrapped in red – a symbol of happiness – and there are plenty of celebrations, especially in Port Louis' Chinatown.

February/March *Maha Shivaratri* A celebration by the Hindu community in honour of Lord Shiva, in which thousands of devotees dressed in white leave their homes in all corners of the island and walk to Grand Bassin, a lake which they believe to be linked to the River Ganges. *Holi* A lively, two-day Hindu festival during which unsuspecting passers-by get squirted with coloured water and powder, which is supposed to bring good luck.

March/April *Ougadi* A low-key New Year festival celebrated by the small minority of Hindu Telegus.

15 August *Assumption Day* Rodrigues' main Christian festival is marked by a vast outdoor mass before the statue of the Virgin Mary at La Reine de Rodrigues, just outside Port Mathurin.

9 September *Anniversary of the death of Père Laval* Mauritians of all denominations walk or drive to the tomb of Père Laval at Sainte-Croix, just outside Port Louis, to celebrate the priest's healing powers.

October/November *Diwali*, or *the Festival of Light* The Hindu community lights the entire island with colourful electric lights (evolving from the traditional small clay lamps and candles), signifying the triumph of good over evil. *Eid al-Fitr* Muslims celebrate the end of Ramadan, the month of fasting. The date varies from year to year according to the lunar calendar, and the exact date depends on the sighting of a full moon.

FOOD AND DRINK

Food lovers are in for a treat in Mauritius, thanks to cuisine as diverse as the country's people. Wherever you dine, you'll find food reflecting influences from India, China, Africa and France, from spicy curries and noodles to a melange of exotic fruit and vegetables, sumptuous seafood, not to mention the basic burger and chips.

Virtually every restaurant has Indian, Chinese, Creole and international food on its menu and if you don't know what to start with, simply ask for *gadjaks*, which are an assortment of hot snacks such as croquettes, *croustillants* (crispy balls) – made from meat, fish, chicken or vegetables – or *gateaux piments* (chilli cakes). Mauritians nibble throughout the day on *gadjaks* and eat large amounts of rice.

Local beef and lamb are less tender than the imported cuts from South Africa, Australia and New Zealand, but home-reared chicken and pork are plentiful and good. With the majority of the population being of the Hindu faith, vegetarians are well catered for. Half the fun of eating out is identifying the fantastic variety of fruit and vegetables.

Croquettes

You can eat cheaply at roadside stalls, stick to your hotel, or venture into the resorts and villages where a range of restaurants dish up tasty meals at knock-down prices at lunchtime. If you are on an all-inclusive deal, try at least a couple of outside restaurants, if only to rub shoulders with the locals and tuck into authentic Mauritian fare. People tend to eat early in the evening and restaurants are often closed by 10pm.

Coquelet tandoori

WHAT TO EAT

Indian

Cooks grind herbs and spices (traditionally on a 'curry rock') to make a masala, which is then used with meat, chicken, fish or vegetables to produce delicious curries. The *vindaye* curries, made from wine, vinegar and garlic, are delicious. Some curries are hotter than others, depending on the ingredients used. Plain boiled or saffron-flavoured rice is always served along with chilli sauce. If the curry is too hot, resist the temptation to drink water; mop up the sauce with rice or bread. Indian bread includes thick rounds of roti (similar to naan), which can be plain or stuffed, or the finer version called *faratha*. Rice-based biryani, flavoured with a subtle blend of spices and spiked with meat, fish, chicken or vegetables, is a typical Muslim dish.

Spices play a major role in both Indian and Creole dishes

Commonly eaten by all Mauritians, *dholl puri* is an Indian snack that is virtually a meal in itself. Best eaten at the roadside stalls found in resorts, villages and markets because it is freshly made to order, these gut-busting floury pancakes are made with crushed lentils and come stuffed with a tomato, onion and garlic-flavoured sauce called *rougaille* and a choice of other traditional fillings. The luminous green chilli sauce is optional, but a smattering gives it that extra bite. *Puris*, conversely, are lighter, tiny disc-shaped pancakes that can be filled with tasty portions of vegetable or meat curry. Also, try *samoussas* (curry-filled pastries) fresh from the pan.

Chinese

Chinese dishes are varied and of excellent value. For something fast, cheap and easy, ask for a *mine frite* (fried noodles). If you're feeling adventurous or especially hungry, ask for a *mine frite special*, which includes eggs, seafood, chicken or meat. A lighter version that is not unlike vermicelli is *meefoon*. Try *bol renversee*, an upturned bowl of rice stabbed with slivers of pork, spicy sausage and chunky chicken, or *fooyang*, an omelette-based offering filled with lobster, crab or prawns. Exotic dishes such as shark-fin soup, sea cucumber and Peking duck are the preserve of upmarket restaurants and should be ordered in advance. Chefs use lots of *ajinomoto* (MSG or monosodium glutamate) to enhance flavour, but you can ask them to use none.

Creole

Creole food is best described as a fiery fusion of Indian, Chinese and French cuisine; it is traditionally spicy. The result depends on the whims and imagination of the cook. Culinary wonders emerge from the cooking pot in the form of rich meat and fish daubes (casseroles) and *caris* (curries), helped along with the ubiquitous chilli and a cornucopia of herbs and spices. Venison and wild boar are especially good in season, and plenty of seafood, including octopus and squid, are served this way, along with a vast variety of local fish, usually grilled or fried. Among the exotic vegetables are *coeur de palmist* (palm hearts), known as millionaire's salad; *gros pois* (butter beans); *brèdes* (fresh greens); and *lentilles noires* (black lentils). Pumpkin and marrow are also popular. As

An upside-down bowl dish

Bounty of the sea

Fish dishes feature strongly in this island nation's cuisine for obvious reasons. Species you may find on the menu include *vieille rouge* (grouper), *carangue* (trevally), *cordonnier* (surgeon fish), *cateaux* (parrot fish), *bourgeois* (red snapper), *capitaine* (white snapper) and *licorne* (unicorn fish). Local specialities to look out for are smoked marlin, *gambas* (native giant prawn), *camaron* (freshwater crayfish) and *crevettes* (a tiny, pricey river shrimp).

an accompaniment, you may be offered *achards légumes* (pickled grated vegetables), which are served in small side dishes.

Desserts

Desserts in restaurants are usually fresh fruits of the season, ice creams or sweet pancakes, or Indian-style, such as kulfi, while hotel buffets include a wide variety of European-style sticky pastries, fancy puddings, cakes and cheeses. Summer fruits include mangoes, lychees, watermelon and passion fruit, and there is plenty of pawpaw, pineapple and banana year-round. Indian sweets are reserved for special occasions, although you can sometimes buy them at patisseries and supermarkets. Small, round waxy cakes called *gateaux cirées* are served at Chinese New Year.

Rodriguan specialities

The lagoons of Rodrigues provide a natural larder for the islanders, most of whom are fisherfolk. Fish and other seafood are served in hotels and local restaurants in Port Mathurin. Octopus is used in salads, *cari* (curry) and *daube* (casserole) and is less expensive than lobster, prawn and crab, which are simply steamed. Another local speciality is *cono cono*, a mollusc similar to whelk, which is incorporated into a refreshing salad dressed with local limes. Fresh fish is jazzed up and fried Chinese style with ginger and garlic. *Cari de poulet aux grains* (chicken curry with red beans) and *poisson salé* (salt fish) are typical Rodriguan dishes served with plain boiled rice. Try to go easy on the local *achards* (pickles) since they are made from considerably stronger chillies than those grown in Mauritius.

Desserts are not really eaten and fresh fruit is rare, but you can find plenty of shops selling *pain frit* (fried bread sprinkled with sugar), *gateau patate* (sweet potato cake), *gateau manioc* (manioc cake) and *pudding maïs* (maize pudding). All drinks, including beer, soft drinks and water, are imported from Mauritius.

WHERE TO EAT

Most luxury hotels tend to be in isolated locations, and dining in local restaurants often involves a taxi ride. Hotel food is plentiful

Fresh produce is readily available

and varied, although often toned down to cater for international tastes. The large hotels often have several restaurants, usually a main buffet-style one and one or more a la carte or beach restaurants. Some hotels have separate facilities, or eating times, for children.

Many local restaurants may seem oddly located, squeezed between, above or behind ramshackle buildings, tucked behind petrol-station forecourts or hidden deep in the cane fields. The decor may be quirky and the service, although friendly and welcoming, may not always come up to international standard. However, the food is fresh and tasty. The more expensive restaurants have air conditioning, tasteful furnishings and often pleasant views.

Most top tourist attractions, such as La Vallée de Ferney, Eureka, L'Aventure du Sucre and Casela Nature Parks, have restaurants set in gorgeous locations. These tend to be favoured by tour groups, but there is nothing to stop you from making a reservation or, in some cases, just turning up.

LUNCH WITH THE LOCALS

In Rodrigues, unlike Mauritius, it is common for locals to prepare and serve lunch to visitors in their own homes. This concept, known as table d'hôte, makes an interesting alternative to restaurant dining and the experience gives a unique insight into local culinary traditions. The food will typically be Rodriguan, such as *cono cono* (a small whelk), octopus curry, or pork in honey served with pulses on a bed of rice, with fiery pickles followed by pancakes or papaya sorbet. Details of participating islanders' homes can be obtained from the Rodrigues Tourism Office (tel: 230 832 0866, www.tourism-rodrigues.mu).

Several colonial houses have been restored to their former grandeur and serve a typical Creole lunch of smoked marlin and palmheart salad, venison or seafood in stylish surroundings. Try Eureka House at Eureka, Table du Chateau at Château de Labourdonnais, and Le Saint Aubin at Bois Cheri. Reservations are recommended.

There are sophisticated Thai, Japanese and Italian restaurants in the Grand Baie area. Fast-food courts in shopping malls also do a roaring trade in local and international fare. Try the food courts at Le Caudan Waterfront in Port Louis, Bagatelle at Reduit, Super U at Grand Baie, and the trendy Ruisseau Creole complex at Tamarin.

DRINKS

Local beers include the Blue Marlin, Stella and Phoenix brands, and craft beer, The Thirsty Fox. Mauritius is one of the few countries in the world that produce industrial and agricultural rum isis, which is often flavoured. Green Island (www.greenislandrum.

Rum treat

If invited into a Mauritian home, you may be offered a glass of *rhum arrangé*, a rum-based concoction in which fruits and spices have been left to macerate for months. It comes in various flavours, from the popular coconut, passion fruit and vanilla, to the more experimental rosemary or chilli.

com) distributes some of the best rums from producers such as New Grove, Chamarel and St Aubin. Some quite palatable red, white and rosé wines are made locally from imported grape concentrate. Labels to look for are Eureka, Chateau Bel Ombre and Saint Nicholas. Australian, New Zealand and South African wines are good value, unlike French wines, champagne and spirits, which can be expensive. A good range of potent alcoholic fruit cocktails is also available, and delicious mocktails.

Non-alcoholic drinks include *alouda*. This is made from *agar agar* (boiled china grass) and sugar, soaked *tookmaria* (sweet basil) seeds and flavoured with milk and rose water. You will also find the usual range of soft drinks and bottled mineral water. Milky, locally-produced vanilla-flavoured tea with plenty of sugar is widely drunk, although black, green and herbal tea is also available. Coffee comes as espresso, filter or cappuccino, but you are more likely to be served with the instant chicory-flavoured version in small snack bars and restaurants.

Finally, it's wise to drink plenty of water. The ubiquitous 'traveller's tummy', blamed so often on 'dodgy' food, is more likely to result from drinking too little water. In Mauritius, especially when it is hot and humid, dehydration is an all too common cause of many stomach complaints, so always carry water. Fortunately, it's plentiful and cheap and can be bought in all food shops and petrol stations.

TO HELP YOU ORDER ...

I would like a table. **Je voudrais une table.**
I'd like a/an/some ... **Je voudrais …**
The bill, please. **L'addition s'il vous plaît.**

bread **pain**
butter **beurre**
coffee **café**
dessert **dessert**
fish **poisson**
fruit **fruit**
ice cream **glace**
meat **viande**
menu **carte**
milk **lait**

pepper **poivre**
potatoes **pommes de terre**
rice **riz**
salad **salade**
salt **sel**
soup **soupe**
sugar **sucre**
tea **thé**
wine **vin**

Bourgeois (red snapper fish)

MENU READER

achards pickled vegetables
agneau lamb
ail garlic
ananas pineapple
bourgeois red snapper fish
brèdes fresh greens
camaron prawns
capitaine white snapper
carangue trevally fish
cari cerf venison curry
cateaux parrot fish
champignons mushrooms
cochon marron wild boar
coeur de palmist palm hearts
cordonnier surgeon fish
crabe crab
daube stewed or casseroled
dessert dessert
entrecote beef rib steak
filet fillet
fruits de mer seafood
gros pois butter beans
haricots beans
jambon ham

kalamar squid
legumes vegetables
lentilles noires black lentils
licorne unicorn fish
marlin fume smoked marlin
melon d'eau watermelon
ourite octopus
petit pois peas
poisson sale salt fish
pommes d'amour tomatoes
poulet/ poisson croustillant crispy fried chicken/fish balls
riz blanc boiled rice
riz saffron saffron-flavoured rice
rougaille tomato, onion and garlic flavoured sauce
sauce piment chilli sauce
saucisse chinoise spicy Chinese sausage
thon tuna
vieille rouge grouper fish
vindaye curry dish based on vinegar or wine and garlic

WHERE TO EAT

We have used the following symbols to give an idea of the cost of a meal for two with soft drinks or beer (imported alcohol can double or even treble the bill). Menu prices do not always include 15 percent VAT, so check first:

$$$$	over R3,000
$$$	R2,000–3,000
$$	R1,000–2,000
$	below R1,000

PORT LOUIS

Brasserie Chic $$$$ *Labourdonnais Waterfront Hotel, tel: 230 202 4000,* www.ninetysixhotels.com. This hotel is Port Louis's foremost address for world-class, cosmopolitan cuisine. The hotel's brassiere-style restaurant serves international cuisine, from bagels to seafood platters, in a friendly, relaxed atmosphere overlooking the harbour.

Côte Jasmin Jardin Bar $$ *9bis Rue St Georges, tel: 230 5798 2573.* With a tranquil garden location at the back of town, this restaurant is noted for its delicious Creole cuisine and its range of cocktails, and live music. Ask for the daily lunch special. Free car parking.

Le Courtyard Restaurant $$$ *corner of St Louis and Chevreau streets, tel: 230 210 0810,* www.le-courtyard.com. An elegant restaurant that welcomes you in the shade of the terrace just in the heart of the bustling city. A favourite among well-heeled locals, it serves delicious French-Mauritian haute cuisine.

The Deck $$$ *Trou Fanfaron Harbour, tel: 230 5928 1111/5940 8005.* Bobbing up and down in the sea on a pontoon dock, The Deck takes seaside dining to a new level. Across from the trendy Caudan promontory, the setting here is much more laid back. The menu demonstrates a French inspiration with an Indian Ocean twist, with shellfish and French fries menu stalwarts.

Restaurant Canton $ *15 Rue Emanuel Anquetil, tel: 230 242 2164*. This long-established restaurant does a roaring trade at lunchtime. Fast service, eclectic decor and a good range of Chinese fare. Last orders for evening meals at 7.30pm.

THE NORTH

Café Muller $ *Royal Road, Grand Baie, tel: 230 263 5230*. This charming family-run German coffee shop tucked behind the main coast road is noted for authentic *stollen*, salads and Saturday brunch. It has a lovely garden setting with a tropical atmosphere.

Chez Tante Athalie $$ *Pamplemousses, tel: 230 243 9266*. Named after the family maid who left behind some secret recipes, this quirky little restaurant has vintage cars in the garden and serves genuine home-cooked Creole food only. For lunch, try the typical *rougaille*, rice, lentils and *brèdes* (greens).

La Cigale $ *Royal Road, Pointe aux Canonniers, tel: 230 263 0193*. With its tables and awnings on the forecourt, this tiny pizzeria is renowned for its delicious home-made pizzas, pasta and meatballs. Finish up with an authentic tiramisu.

Cokoloko $$ *B13 Grand Baie, tel: 230 263 1241,* https://cocoloko.net. This popular restaurant and pizzeria lies across the road from Grand Baie public beach. Italian, French, Indian and Spanish cuisines feature on the menu, along with seafood and a good dessert list. A roster of live music enlivens the restaurant on weekends. There's a four-hour 'happy hour' every day.

L'Escale $$ *Route Bois Cheri, Moka. tel: 230 5422 2332,* http://escalecreole.net. Set in a lovely tropical garden in Moka and decorated with reams of Mauritian memorabilia, this is the place to sample authentic Mauritian cuisine. Run by a mother and daughter team, the service is as charming as the location, and *sega* classics play as you eat. Choose from good value 'Creole', 'Discovery' and 'Gourmet' set lunch menus. Reservation recommended.

Le Fangourin $$ *Beau Plan, Pamplemousses, tel: 230 243 7900,* http://aventure dusucre.com. Overlooking manicured gardens, this charming a la carte restaurant is well placed as a lunch stop if you visit L'Aventure du Sucre Museum. It serves extensive Creole and European fare and is renowned for delicious desserts using local speciality sugars.

Foley's Restaurant $ *Royal Road, 7th mile, Triolet, tel: 230 261 4533*. For typical Mauritian cuisine of biryani, noodles or curry, this no-frills restaurant on the main road is renowned for good value, friendly service, not to mention great cocktails.

Happy Rajah $$ *Super U, Royal Road, tel: 230 263 2241,* http://happyrajah. com. A hot favourite for authentic South Indian food. Good range of vegetarian and meat dishes, and accommodating staff. Try the selection of naan bread with vegetable *makhanwala*. There is also decent coffee and Indian desserts. Handy off-street parking.

La Pescatore $$$ *Coastal Road, Trou aux Biches, tel: 230 265 6337,* www.le pescatore.com. This a la carte restaurant is one of the finest on the island, serving delectable seafood dishes in a beach house on the water. The interior is contemporary, with marine-inspired colour, and in the evening, diners can enjoy a sunset cocktail on the jetty. The set menus are good value. Reservations recommended.

Restaurant Coolen Chez Ram $ *Coast Road, Grand Baie, tel: 230 263 8569*. One of the few restaurants in the area that is always buzzing with tourists and locals. The welcoming owner and staff serve typical Mauritian cuisine.

Restaurant Souvenir $ *Coastal Road, Trou aux Biches, tel: 230 5291 1440*. Across the road from the police station and popular with beachgoers for a casual drink or snack. Tuck into chop suey, fried noodles or fish and meat curries.

La Table du Château $$ *Domaine de Labourdonnais, Mapou, tel: 230 266 7172,* www.tableduchateau.com. Seasonal produce from the estate is weaved into old family recipes at this smart gastronomic restaurant on the grounds of Château de Labourdonnais, which is open-sided in summer. Book a tasting at the adjacent Rum Bar. Dinner reservations are recommended.

Le Tandoor $$ *Royal Road, Grand Baie, tel: 230 263 1378*. A traditional Indian restaurant with bursts of colour and equipped with a genuine tandoor oven, which gives the food cooked in it an extra-tasty, deep flavour.

Weiner Walzer Café $$ *Powder Mills Road, Pamplemousses, tel: 230 243 8465*. Situated roughly 100m (109yd) from the gate of the Botanical Gardens, this cosy, rustic café offers colonial-style decor, wooden tables and wicker chairs, a peasant ambience and a decent range of food options, including good desserts.

THE EAST

Chez Manuel $$$ *Royal Road, St Julien Village, Union Flacq, tel: 230 418 3599*. There's a nice buzz and pleasant service in this restaurant, which has lots of dining alcoves in a garden setting. The food is not cheap, but if you're staying on the east coast, dining at Chez Manuel is well worth the taxi fare to get there. Specialities include Chinese and Creole food, grills and seafood. **Chez Tino $$** *Royal Road, Trou d' Eau Douce, tel: 230 480 2769,* https://chez-tino-restaurant.business.site. Serves excellent authentic Creole dishes, fresh seafood and also noodle plates. The house specialty is Mauritian paella.

Le Jardin de Beau Vallon $$$ *Beau Vallon, Mahébourg, tel: 230 631 2850*. This 100-year-old colonial house is a ten-minute drive from the airport and was rescued from rack and ruin by the present owners, who have faithfully restored it to its former glory. The shaded dining veranda, wooden floors and antique furniture reflect a bygone era. Surrounded by lush gardens of tropical fruit and trees, it's the place to enjoy Creole specialities such as octopus and green pawpaw curry. Good wine list, excellent service and a private parking area. Reservations recommended.

Symon's $$ *Coastal Road, Poste de Flacq, Belle Mare, tel: 230 415 1135,* https://symon-restaurant.business.site. It's well worth forgoing your hotel restaurant to come to this pleasant place where you can enjoy local food in a local setting. Seafood, Creole and Chinese food are served inside or on the terrace.

THE SOUTH

Le Batelage $$ *Port Souillac, Savanne, tel: 230 625 6084*. A former warehouse on the banks of the Savanne River has been converted into an attractive restaurant with a large sheltered terrace. The menu offers European and Creole dishes. The service is generally unhurried, but the laid-back atmosphere changes when tour groups arrive.

Le Chamarel Restaurant $$$ *La Crete, Chamarel, tel: 230 483 4421,* www.lechamarelrestaurant.com. Rustic-style restaurant offering typical Mauritian cuisine in a gorgeous hillside setting overlooking Île aux Benitiers and the lagoons of the southwest. It's a popular lunch stop for tour groups exploring the nearby Chamarel Coloured Earths and a good place to try local specialities.

Le Château de Bel Ombre $$$$ *Bel Ombre, tel: 230 623 5522,* www.lechateaudebelombre.com.This magnificent, upmarket restaurant occupies a magnificently restored colonial house in a spectacular setting overlooking landscaped gardens. Enjoy a gourmet lunch or romantic dinner with a sundowner or wine tasting with the sommelier. Reservations recommended.

Chez Rosy $$ *Gris Gris, Souillac, tel: 230 625 4179.* This small, unpretentious – and reasonably priced – clifftop restaurant is famous for its fresh lobster, which is prepared in various ways, from grilled to curried. It also serves typical Mauritian specialities.

The Hungry Crocodile Restaurant $$ *La Vanille Nature Park, Rivière des Anguilles, tel: 230 626 2503,* www.lavanille-naturepark.com. Feeling hungry after watching the crocs feed in this nature park? On the menu is an exotic range of Mauritian dishes, including crocodiles served in various ways, fritters, curry or kebabs in this restaurant overlooking a forested valley. The less adventurous can opt for the croc-free croque-monsieur.

Le Saint Aubin Restaurant $$ *Rivière des Anguilles, Savanne, tel: 230 626 1513,* www.saintaubinloisirs.com. Step back in time at this handsome nineteenth-century plantation house near the Bois Cheri tea plantation. Enjoy a leisurely lunch of typical Mauritian and Creole dishes on the open veranda overlooking the lovely gardens. The house and restaurant are popular with tour groups exploring the tea route. Reservations are essential.

Varangue-sur-Morne $$$ *110 Plaine Champagne Rd, Chamarel, tel: 230 483 5710.* Fabulous lunch location overlooking undulating cane fields with views of Île aux Benitiers. Timber stairways lead down to a charming restaurant in tropical gardens specialising in Creole and European fare, including seasonal game. Ideal if exploring the Black River Gorges. This spot is popular with tour groups, so you should book ahead.

Wapalapam $$$, *Le Morne Brabant. tel: 230 5852 2902,* http://wapalapam. com. This boho-chic eatery has one of the most creative menus on the island. There's an eclectic blend of cuisine from the Indian Ocean. You can order small sharing plates to discover different flavours, and there's a good selection of wines. Much of the decor is handmade or recycled, from the pirogues out front to the tables and cutlery. Reservations are recommended for dinner.

THE WEST

Big Willy's $$ *Le Barachois, Tamarin, tel: 230 483 7400,* www.bigwillys.mu. Fashionable hang-out with a pleasant outdoor terrace with live sports on a big screen. Serves European and Creole food, and the menu changes regularly. During the evening, the space transforms into a trendy pub-cum-club. Opens late on Wed, Fri & Sat.

Creole Shack $ *Radar Avenue, Flic en Flac, tel: 230 5736 1523.* Good-value food can be found at this tiny rustic eatery; the female owner cooks an authentic traditional three-course Mauritian meal. Reservations recommended.

Domaine Anna $$$ *Morcellement Anna, Medine, Flic en Flac, tel: 230 453 9650,* https://domaineanna.mu. Upmarket Chinese food is served at this vast circular restaurant built from local stone. For romantic dining, ask for a private waterside pavilion. Specialities include seafood with palm-heart salad and steamed fish and ginger. It gets busy at the weekend, so book ahead.

Le Kiosk $ *Ruisseau Creole, Black River, tel: 230 483 7*004, www.ruisseaucreole. com. Try the fresh croissants and coffee or grab a croque-monsieur in this alfresco eatery after a spot of retail therapy in the nearby designer shopping complex. Opens late Fri–Sun.

Pakbo $$ *Royal Road, Flic en Flac, tel: 230 5380 7258.* Neat little boho-chic eatery serving curry and great upside-down bowl dishes. They also have an excellent selection of seafood options.

Restaurant Pavillon de Jade $$ *Trois Bras Store, Royal Road, Black River, tel: 230 483 6151.* This atmospheric Chinese restaurant on a first-floor terrace opposite the entrance to Black River National Park makes an ideal place to fill up before or after a long walk.

PLATEAU TOWNS

Grain D'Sel Restaurant $$ *Hennessy Park Hotel, 65 Ebène Cybercity, Ebène, tel: 230 403 7200,* https://ninetysixhotels.com. A fashionable yet cosy restaurant decorated with black and white photographs taken by local artists. Fresh local produce is blended with an array of island and oriental spices in contemporary creative cuisine.

King Dragon $$ *St Jean Road, Quatre Bornes, tel: 230 424 7888,* https://king-dragon.mu. One of the local favourite restaurants, owned by the same family as Domaine Anna. The expertly prepared menu boasts Chinese Mauritian cuisine at its finest. King prawns are their speciality. Booking is advised as it is usually packed at the weekends.

Meltin' Potes $ *Moka Business Park, Moka, tel: 230 433 8105.* This trendy bistro provides all-day snacks and French-style meals in a clean, modern setting. It's a popular place for lunch due to the excellent sandwiches, paninis and fries.

La Potiniere $$$ *Rue Charles Lees, Curepipe, tel: 230 6702648,* www.lapotiniere.mu. In the heart of the Corson tea fields, this classy, cosy restaurant in a chic factory setting, complete with a wood burner, sitting area and bar, specialises in game dishes and French and Creole cuisine. The staff are helpful and professional.

RODRIGUES

L'Atelier Gourmand $ *Rue François Leguat, tel: 230 5496 0714.* This restaurant on a first-floor terrace has a great location and specialises in delicious local and French cuisine.

Le Marlin Bleu $$ *Anse aux Anglais, tel: 230 832 0701/5252 2246.* Come here for tasty seafood salads and a mix of other seafood, pizza and local dishes – something for everyone.

TRAVEL ESSENTIALS

PRACTICAL INFORMATION

A

ACCOMMODATION

Branded hotels in Mauritius are ranked according to an international star-rating system, and those owned by Mauritian groups are classified by an island star system that approximately allies with this. Most hotels featured by overseas tour operators undergo frequent maintenance and refurbishment and are of a generally high standard, with service to match. All beach hotels offer complimentary watersports, except for big-game fishing, scuba diving and kitesurfing, and many have diving schools, land sports such as tennis (and increasingly padel), and often golf on site or nearby, a spa and a gym.

Hotels owned and managed by companies such as Beachcomber (www.beachcomber-hotels.com), Constance (www.constancehotels.com), The LUX Collective (www.theluxcollective.com), Sunlife (www.yoursunlife.com), Attitude (https://hotels-attitude.com/en) and Veranda (www.veranda-resorts.com) are in stunning, often isolated, beach locations, while Ninety-Six Hotels (https://ninetysixhotels.com) (previously Indigo Hotels) operates glamorous city and business hotels.

Increasingly popular with repeat visitors is staying in self-catering accommodation in the main resorts of Grand Baie and Flic en Flac. Generally, the rate you pay depends on the distance from the beach and/or your length of stay; the cheapest options are for units some distance from the beach rented for long periods. While these units should be registered with the tourist office, many are not, and you may find that fundamental safety and security measures don't meet Western standards. Always inspect the rooms before committing yourself. Three reputable companies in Mauritius with a wide selection of accommodation are Horizon Holidays (www.horizon.mu), Mauritours (www.mauritours.mu) and Muse Villas (https://musevillas.com) and in the UK, Elegant Destinations (www.elegantdestinations.co.uk). Many properties on the island can be booked via platforms such as Booking.com (www.booking.com) and Airbnb (www.airbnb.com).

Visitors wanting something other than the sun, sea and sand should look for eco-lodges and traditional rural bungalows. Some useful websites to visit

include   www.lavieillecheminee.com,   www.saintaubinloisirs.com,   https://
otentic.mu/en and https://andrea-lodges.com.

There are no official camping sites.

AIRPORT (see also Getting there)

Sir Seewoosagur Ramgoolam International Airport, locally referred to as SSR
(https://mauritius-airport.atol.aero, tel: 230 603 8000), is at Plaine Magnien
near Plaisance, 48km (30 miles) south of the capital, Port Louis. Allow at least
one hour to get there by taxi. If you are on a package holiday, your tour rep
will meet you and arrange a transfer to your hotel. There are no direct buses
to the tourist resorts, so independent travellers will have to take a taxi. Agree
on a fare before accepting a ride, and expect to pay around R2,700 for the
journey to Grand Baie.

Helicopter transfers from the airport to your hotel take fifteen minutes
and can take up to a maximum of four people. Air Mauritius Helicopters
(tel: 230 603 3754, http://airmauritius.com/mauritius-helicopter-ltd) charge
R28,000 for two people (R4,000 per additional person), while more spacious
Corail Helicopters (tel: 230 261 2266; https://corailhelico-mu.com/en) charge
R60,000 per helicopter.

B

BICYCLE HIRE

Bicycles and helmets – and increasingly electric bikes – in good condition
can be rented from the more upmarket hotels. Hotels can also organise
guided cycle tours of the island and provide helmets, particularly in the quieter south and east, which lends themselves to some easy rides. Most resorts
have bikes for hire but check brakes, gears and tyres as they are not always in
good condition. Punctures can be easily repaired at a tyre repair shop in most
villages. Rent mountain bikes, fat bikes and electric bikes (from £25 per day,
plus delivery charge) from specialists DunienZil (tel: 230 5828 8685, https://
explorenouzil.com/en/bike-rental-in-mauritius), who also offer guided tours
island-wide.

BUDGETING FOR YOUR TRIP

Expect to pay handsomely for all those extras if you confine yourself to a hotel. In the real world, basics are remarkably cheap and nearly everything is paid for in Mauritian rupees, although debit and credit cards are accepted in many shops. Approximately £1 is worth 57 rupees and US$1 is worth around 44 rupees.

Getting there. Despite an open-skies policy, airfares are a significant expense, especially if coming from Europe or the US. Package deals through a tour operator can sometimes work out only fractionally higher than the airfare.

Accommodation. The sky's the limit at the posh beach-resort hotels where you can expect to pay European prices and more. A mid-range hotel costs around R5,000 a night for a double room with breakfast and dinner. Self-catering options are very good value, from R3,000 a day for an apartment or villa.

Meals and drinks. Eating out is cheaper than hotel dining. A simple meal, soft drink, or beer can cost less than R400 per person. Meals in the most expensive non-hotel restaurants are similar to European prices. Seafood, excluding lobster, is plentiful and cheap. Imported alcohol and wine can double the bill.

Local transport. Prices for short taxi journeys are on a par with UK prices, although better deals can be struck for half-day (R2,000) or full-day hire (R3,000–4,000). Buses are cheap and plentiful, if unpredictable and time-consuming, but in resort areas, they stop operating after 7pm. The Metro Express (tel: 230 460 0460, https://mauritiusmetroexpress.mu) is modern, cheap and fast and travels from Curepipe to Aapravasi Ghat via the plateau towns and Port Louis for the same price as the bus.

Museums. Apart from government-owned museums, there is an entry fee with higher tariffs for non-residents. Expect to pay between R100 and R300 for adults. There are reductions for children.

Watersports. Scuba-diving packages of five and ten dives are around R6,000 and R10,000, respectively. Experienced divers can expect to pay around R1,800 for a day dive and R2,000 for a night dive. A day on a big-game fishing boat costs around R21,000. It's always worth asking for discounts. Resort hotel guests can expect free watersports, including windsurfing, snorkelling, SUP and often water skiing and Hobie Cats.

C

CAR HIRE (see also Driving)

Car hire starts from about R1,500 a day. Rates include insurance, collision damage waiver and discounts depending on length of hire. Credit cards are accepted and you will be asked to sign a blank voucher for the deposit, which will be destroyed in your presence when you return the car. Cars can be collected at the airport or any pre-arranged point and dropped off when you leave. The more expensive companies are the international ones such as Avis (tel: 230 637 3100, www.avis.com), Europcar (tel: 230 637 3240, www.europcar.com) and Hertz (tel: 230 604 3000, www.hertz.mu). Less expensive operators include Allo Car (tel: 230 5773 3536, https://allo carrental.com), JR Car Rental (tel: 230 525 10250) and Tropicar (tel: 230 465 9200, www.tropicar.mu).

CLIMATE

Mauritius has a tropical maritime climate. There are two seasons, summer and winter. Summer, from November to April, is hot and humid, with short bursts of heavy rain and the occasional cyclone. Winter, from May to October, is pleasant and dry, nights are cooler and there is less humidity than in summer. The southeast trade winds blow all year, keeping the south and east coasts fresher during the summer, but it can get uncomfortably windy at other times. On the coast, expect daytime temperatures of 20–25°C (68–77°F) in winter and 25–34°C (77–93°F) in summer.

The chart below shows maximum average daytime temperatures in Port Louis.

	J	F	M	A	M	J	J	A	S	O	N	D
°C	30	29	29	28	26	24	24	24	25	27	28	29
°F	86	84	84	82	79	75	75	75	77	81	82	84

Cyclones. The cyclone season is between December and April. Cyclones, powerful tropical storms, start hundreds of kilometres away to the northeast of Mauritius and take days to move westwards. Weather stations in the Indian Ocean track their route, and warnings are broadcast days in advance. Cyclones vary in strength, some merely bringing heavy rains and winds, but others can have devastating effects, resulting in damage to buildings and cuts to the power and water supply, and occasionally, deaths. All hotels have their own generators and are well-equipped to deal with a cyclone. You should not venture out when red warning flags are flown from public buildings. Local radio and TV stations broadcast regular bulletins. For cyclone information, dial 8996 from any Mauritian landline or 171 from a local mobile.

CLOTHING

Loose cotton shorts, shirts, T-shirts and dresses are ideal for the balmy climate of Mauritius. Men should wear a collared shirt, trousers and closed shoes at dinner in upmarket hotels; a jacket and tie are necessary only for formal functions. Wearing swimsuits in the hotel dining room or town is likely to offend, while nudity and topless bathing on any beach is not permitted. A sturdy pair of walking shoes or boots is essential if you intend to go rock climbing or hiking on the island. Sarongs or *pareo* for the beach can be bought from local beach vendors or hotel or resort shops.

CRIME AND SAFETY

Mauritius is a generally low-risk destination. Any crime is usually opportunistic, so avoid deserted, unlit areas, wear a money belt if visiting the Port Louis market, don't flaunt expensive jewellery and don't give lifts to strangers. Women shouldn't walk around alone at night. If driving, never leave anything on show in your car and remember to lock doors and windows in self-catering accommodation. All hotels provide free safety deposit boxes. Do not leave money, jewellery, laptops or cameras on show when you leave your hotel room unattended, even for a few minutes. If you should become a victim of a crime, report the details to the police immediately and insist on a copy of the report or reference number for your insurance purposes.

Sadly, there is one 'no-go area', the slum settlement of Karo Kalyptus, just north of the capital, Port Louis. Motorists have been victims of nasty attacks when forced to slow down on the motorway at the adjacent Roches Bois roundabout.

D

DRIVING

Driving regulations. Drivers should be over 23 and must always carry an international or valid driving licence from their own country to avoid incurring a hefty fine. Driving is on the left. Speed limits are 90km/h (60mph) on the motorway and 50km/h (30mph) elsewhere. Distances and speed limits are shown in kilometres and road signs are in English. The wearing of seatbelts is compulsory and there is no age restriction for front-seat passengers. Parking restrictions apply in towns and you should display a parking coupon, available in booklets from petrol stations. If you hire a motorcycle, you must wear a crash helmet. Accidents should be reported on an 'agreed statement of facts' form provided with your hire car. Personal injury accidents must be reported to the police.

Be warned: Driving in Mauritius is not for the faint-hearted due to badly lit streets, poorly placed road signs, an absence of decent pavements and incompetent driving habits.

Fuel. Most filling stations are open from 7am to 10pm, but some are open 24 hours on the motorway near residential areas. Prices for petrol and diesel are on a par with those in Europe. Petrol costs about R40 per litre. Attendants will fill your car and do not expect a tip. Ensure you have cash, as credit cards are only accepted in some places.

E

ELECTRICITY

Electrical appliances in hotels operate on 220 volts. Both square three-pin plugs and round two-pin plugs are used on the island but take an adaptor.

EMBASSIES AND CONSULATES

Australia: Rogers House (2nd floor), 5 John Kennedy St, Port Louis, tel: 230 202 0160, www.mauritius.embassy.gov.au.

Canada: 3 Royal St, Sir Jean Moilin Court, Port Louis, tel: 230 5500 2808, www.international.gc.ca/country-pays/mauritius-maurice/port_louis. aspx?lang=eng#contact

New Zealand: Anse Courtois, Les Pailles, tel: 230 286 4920, www.safetravel. govt.nz/mauritius.

South Africa: 4th floor, BAI Building, 25 Pope Hennessy St, Port Louis, tel: 230 212 6925, www.gov.za.

UK: Sir Hesketh Bell Street, Plaines Wilhems, tel: 230 660 4900. There is also an Honorary Consul in Port Mathurin, Rodrigues, tel: 230 832 0120. www.gov.uk/world/organisations/british-high-commission-port-louis

US: 4th Floor, Rogers House, John Kennedy Street, Port Louis, tel: 230 202 4400, https://mu.usembassy.gov.

EMERGENCIES (see also Medical care and Police)

The following numbers are helpful 24 hours a day in an emergency:

Police **999**

Fire **115**

Ambulance **114**

G

GETTING THERE (see also Airport)

Most visitors arrive in Mauritius on a packaged scheduled airline deal provided by their home travel agent or tour operator. Scheduled flights with the national carrier, Air Mauritius (www.airmauritius.com), come from Europe, Africa, Asia and Australia. Travellers from the US will need to take a connecting flight. Air Mauritius flies directly from the following destinations: London, Paris, Geneva, Johannesburg, Cape Town, Réunion, Rodrigues, Kuala Lumpur, Mumbai, Delhi and Perth, and to over fifty destinations with airline partners. Fares from the UK start at around £580.

The only way of getting to Rodrigues is by air or sea from Mauritius or the French island of Réunion. The flight with Air Mauritius (www.airmauritius. com) takes about an hour and a half and should be booked well ahead, especially in peak season.

From Mauritius, it is possible to travel by sea, although this isn't recommended for anyone but the hardiest independent travellers. Contact the Mauritius Shipping Corporation (tel: 230 217 2285, www.mauritius shipping.net).

A French charter company, Corsair (www.flycorsair.com), flies from Paris to Mauritius. Other airlines serving Mauritius are Air Austral (www.air-austral.com), British Airways (www.britishairways.com), Air France (www. airfrance.com), Emirates (www.emirates.com), Condor (www.condor.com), South African Airways (www.flysaa.com) and Air Seychelles (www.air seychelles.com).

GUIDES AND TOURS

If you're staying in an isolated hotel and want to see the island, booking a guided tour is best. Local tour operators, such as Mauritours (tel: 230 467 9700, https:// mauritours.mu), Mautourco (tel: 230 604 3000, https://mautourco.com) and Summertimes (tel: 230 427 1111, https://summer-times.com) have hospitality desks at major hotels and can arrange full- and half-day tours in air-conditioned vehicles with multilingual guides, as well as sea excursions, helicopter trips and other services.

Smaller companies operate in the resort areas, but you should avoid freelance 'guides' on the beaches and attractions because they won't have appropriate insurance.

Air Mauritius Helicopters (tel: 230 603 3754, http://airmauritius.com/ helicopter.htm) offers regular sightseeing tours. Prices vary depending on flying time and route. Current tariffs start at R20,000 per helicopter for two people (R4,000 per additional person), which can accommodate up to four people. A scenic flight in a modern H120 (Colibri) Corail Helicopters (tel: 230 261 2266; https://corailhelico-mu.com/en) starts from R5000 for a 10-minute 'Heli-Sunset' for two.

H

HEALTH AND MEDICAL CARE

Mauritius is malaria-free and no vaccinations are needed unless coming from an infected area. Taking out travel insurance is a good idea, but remember that many companies exclude coverage for extreme sports, such as rock climbing and mountaineering. However, you may be covered for quad biking. If you are contemplating participating in sea or land sports, confirm with the tour operator that the activity is within your level, keeping in mind that the operator is in business to make money. You should ask your guide to confirm that they are qualified first-aider and that drinks and first-aid equipment are always carried. But most importantly – and this cannot be stressed enough – ask what emergency backup measures exist in case of accident or sudden illness. Emergency medical treatment is no longer free in public hospitals, these tend to be overcrowded and understaffed, and ambulances are poorly equipped. If there is any doubt at all, don't book.

Plenty of good private clinics recognise overseas travel-insurance policies, so keep all receipts and documentation in the event of a medical claim. Emergency and/or routine treatment costs substantially less than in Europe. If you need a doctor or dentist, consult your hotel. Most generic medicines are available at pharmacies, which are recognisable by a green cross, but if you are on any special medication, it is better to bring your own.

Tap water is said to be safe to drink, except during water shortages or cyclone periods, but few visitors drink it, and even the locals boil it. Plenty of bottled water is available, increasingly in recyclable glass bottles at hotels. Tummy upsets should be rare since hotel food is prepared under strict hygienic conditions.

Wear protective shoes when exploring the reef and muddy waters. If you should tread on the venomous stonefish, seek medical treatment immediately.

Public hospitals. SSR Hospital, Pamplemousses (tel: 230 243 9407); S Bharati Eye Hospital, Moka (tel: 230 433 3449); Doctor Jeetoo Hospital,

Port Louis (tel: 230 212 3201); Princess Margaret Hospital, Quatre Bornes (tel: 230 425 3031); Jawaharlal Nehru Hospital, Rose Belle (tel: 230 627 3118), Victoria Hospital, Candos (tel: 230 427 4535), Mahébourg Hospital (tel: 230 604 2000). **Private clinics and hospitals** accepting medical insurance are Clinique du Nord, Pamplemousses (tel: 230 247 1056, www.cliniquedunord. mu); C-Care Darné, Floréal (tel: 230 601 2300, www.cliniquedarne.com), C-Care Wellkin Hospital (tel: 230 605 1000, www.wellkinhospital.com) and clinics in Grand Baie and Tamarin; Medpoint Hospital and clinic, Quatre Bornes (tel: 230 426 7777); Clinique de Grand Baie (tel: 230 263 1212, www. cliniquedegrandbaie.com).

L

LANGUAGE

The official language is English, although most people are more comfortable conversing in French. Creole, a form of pidgin French, remains the lingua franca. You'll also hear Indian and Chinese languages spoken, such as Hindi, Bhojpuri (a sort of Creolised Hindi), Tamil, Urdu, Telegu, Marathi, Gujarati, Mandarin and Cantonese. Nearly everyone employed in tourism speaks both English and French.

LGBTQ+ TRAVELLERS

Homosexuality is illegal in Mauritius but tolerated. However, open displays of affection between same-sex couples may draw unwanted attention and cat-calling. The island's hotels and resorts are more open and welcome same-sex couples, so you shouldn't experience problems there.

M

MAPS

The tourist office produces a free map, and other reasonable ones can be found in hotel shops. *Ile Maurice,* published by the Institute of Geographic National, costs around R500 and can be bought in any bookshop. Alternatively, the French IGN Road Map 85001 or the Mauritius-Rodrigues Michelin Road Map 740 (updated in 2023). Both maps are available in the UK at Stanford's, 12/14 Long Acre, Covent Garden, London WC2E 9LP, tel: 020 7836 1321, www.stanfords.co.uk.

MEDIA

For a country whose official language is English, there are surprisingly few publications in English. What books there are tend to be imported and expensive, and current magazines and newspapers are often hard to come by. All local newspapers are in French and include *Le Matinal*, *The Independent*, *Defi Quotidien* (daily), *Defi Plus* (weekly) and *L'Express*, which has one article in English on Thursdays.

The top hotels provide satellite and digital TV. The Mauritius Broadcasting Corporation (MBC) transmits television news in English at 9am and 9pm. You can also get BBC news, Al Jazeera and other channels, and radio news at 8am, 3pm and 9pm daily. Many expatriate households subscribe to South African-based DSTV, with daily English language programs. On the radio, the BBC World Service is broadcast all day on 1575AM. Local radio stations focusing on pop music, interviews and items of local interest are Radio 1 on 101.7FM, Radio Plus on 88.6FM and Top FM on 105.7FM.

MONEY

Currency. The currency used is the Mauritian rupee (R). Notes are in denominations of 25, 50, 100, 200, 500, 1,000 and 2,000; coins are R1, R5 and R20 and 5, 10, 20 and 50 cents. There is no restriction on the amount of foreign currency you can bring to the country, but if you have a surplus of rupees on departure, you can convert them to your home currency. Keep all bank receipts, as you can only export a maximum of R350.

Currency exchange. The rupee is a fluctuating currency, so keep an eye on the daily exchange rates. Many banks in Grand Baie, Curepipe, Port Louis and at the airport offer much better deals on major currencies than in your hotel or through official money-changing shops.

Credit cards. Major credit cards are accepted in large supermarkets, more expensive shops and restaurants, hotels and car hire companies. Many retail outlets display credit card symbols but always check that they take your card before purchasing. Some petrol stations do not accept credit cards at all. Be aware of the high costs charged by your bank or credit card company when using plastic abroad.

ATMs. ATMs are found at banks, supermarkets and shopping malls.

O

OPENING TIMES

Shops: Shops in Port Louis are open weekdays 9am–5pm and Saturdays 9am–noon. In the plateau towns, most shops close at noon on Thursdays. Port Louis Municipal Market is open Monday to Saturday 6am–6pm and Sunday 6am–noon. The small corner shops or boutiques are open daily 6am–6pm.

Businesses and offices: Weekdays 8am–4.30pm; some businesses are open Saturday morning from 9am–noon. Government offices are open weekdays 9am–4pm, but are closed for lunch between 11.15am and noon.

Banks: Monday–Thursday 9am–3.30pm; Friday 9am–4pm. Closed Saturday and Sunday.

Museums: Hours vary greatly. Some close for one or two days a week and at weekends. Check before making a long journey.

Restaurants: Restaurants do not keep late hours and last orders should be made before 9pm. Many close on Mondays.

P

POLICE

Most police officers in Mauritius are friendly and keen to help visitors to the island. English is spoken at all police stations and there are specially trained tourist police in Grand Baie. Police Headquarters are at Line Barracks, Port Louis, tel: 468 0034; http://police.gov.mu.

The police generally leave tourists alone, but if you are driving, always carry your licence in case of random checks. There is also a strong presence of police on the 'motorway' where speeding is common and offenders are instantly reported.

POST OFFICES

In Mauritius, post offices are the only place to buy stamps and post letters. Registered parcels to overseas destinations are checked before being sent, so don't seal them until presenting them at the post-office counter. The price for sending a small postcard anywhere in the world is R32. Mail for other destinations should be weighed. Delivery usually takes between seven and ten days. Customs always check parcels received in Mauritius from overseas and these must be collected in person at Parcel Post Office, Quay Street, Port Louis (tel: 230 213 4813); remember to take your passport with you.

There are six post offices in Port Louis. The main post office is on Quay Street (tel: 230 208 2851, www.mauritiuspost.mu). Post offices are open weekdays 8.15am–4pm; Saturdays 8am–11.45am. While there, it's worth popping into the Postal Museum, one of the oldest buildings on the Port Louis waterfront, which tells the history of philately in Mauritius (Mon–Fri 9.30am–4.30pm, Sat & Public Holidays 9.30am–3.30pm; charge; tel: 230 213 4812).

PUBLIC HOLIDAYS

The following are public holidays when all public services are closed:
1 and 2 January New Year's Day
1 February Abolition of Slavery Day
12 March Republic Day
1 May Labour Day
1 November All Saints' Day
2 November Arrival of the Indentured Labourers
25–26 December Christmas and Boxing Day
In addition, the various religions celebrate eight major festivals, mostly with moveable dates. The date of Eid al-Fitr, marking the end of Ramadan, varies

from year to year according to the lunar calendar and over time, can take place in any month.

January/February Chinese Spring Festival

Mid-January/February Cavadee

February/March Maha Shivaratri; Holi

March/April Ougadi; Easter

15 August Assumption Day

September Ganesh Chaturthi

October/November Diwali

On Rodrigues, Chinese-run shops and businesses shut down for about one week during the Chinese Spring Festival.

R

RELIGION

Just under half the population (49 percent) are Hindu, 32 percent are Christian, predominantly Roman Catholic, some 17 percent practise Islam and 0.4% are Buddhists. Some religious festivals are also public holidays and reflect the religious tolerance of Mauritius's multicultural society. Remove your shoes and cover your arms and legs when visiting temples or mosques. In Rodrigues, the main religion is Roman Catholicism, with most churches being in Port Mathurin (where there is also a Hindu temple and a mosque).

Services in English are held as follows: Roman Catholic Mass on Saturday at Notre Dames de Lourdes, Sir, Celicourt Antelme Street, Rose Hill (tel: 230 464 3422) and at St Anne Catholic Church, 18 St Anne's Rd, Beau Bassin (tel: 230 464 1930); Church of England service the last Sunday of each month at 9.15 at St Clement Church, St Clements Street, Curepipe (tel: 230 676 2250) and ad hoc services in English at St Paul's Church, La Caverne, Vacoas (tel: 230 584 30727); Presbyterian service at 9.30am every Sunday at St Columba's Church, 23 Palmerston Rd, Phoenix (tel: 234 697 8394, www.presbyterian.mu). On Rodrigues, St Barnabas Church in Jenner Street holds an English-language service once a month on Sundays at 8.30am.

T

TELEPHONES

Roaming services are available through my.t (www.myt.mu/mobile) and Emtel (www.emtel.com) networks, which can also supply local SIM cards if you plan to stay longer. You must produce passport identification and wait at least one working day to be connected. As in the rest of the world, if you use your hotel phone, you will incur hefty surcharges.

For international mobile phone rental in Mauritius, see www.cellular abroad.com/rentals-mauritius.php. If you're staying a while and are likely to be making many local calls, you may want to consider investing in an inexpensive SIM-only local phone. Credit can be added and topped up by buying phone cards in supermarkets and small shops.

The international dialling code for Mauritius and Rodrigues is 230. To call home from Mauritius and/or Rodrigues, dial the international dialling code, 020, followed by your country code, the area code and then the local number, omitting any initial zero.

Local landline numbers have seven digits (eight for mobiles prefixed with a 5). Simply dial the number for the connection. In case of difficulty or if you need directory enquiries, contact the operator on 150.

TIME ZONES

Mauritius is four hours ahead of Greenwich Mean Time (GMT).

New York	London	Jo'burg	**Mauritius**	Sydney
7am	noon	2pm	**4pm**	10pm

TIPPING

Tipping is not compulsory, but if you have received good service, tips will be appreciated, and it is customary to give a small tip for luggage services, housekeeping, etc, in luxury hotels. A service charge of 10 percent is usually included in restaurant bills; ask if you need clarification. Airport porters are not allowed to take tips. Taxi drivers do not expect tips.

TOILETS

Public toilets have improved in recent years, but there are still some pretty dire ones at bus stations and markets, which should only be used in emergencies. The best of the bunch is inside the Le Caudan Waterfront complex in Port Louis and those found in big supermarkets and shopping complexes. Most public beaches also have adequate toilets. You can always use the toilet in a café or restaurant in emergencies. Carrying a supply of toilet paper is highly recommended.

TOURIST INFORMATION

Official tourist information can be obtained by visiting https://mauritiusnow.com. The Mauritius Tourism Promotion Authority (MTPA) representation offices abroad include the following:

Australia: Mauritius High Commission, 2 Beale Crescent, Deakin, Canberra, ACT 2600 (tel: 020 612 6281 1203, https://mauritius-canberra.govmu.org).

UK: MMGY-Hills Balfour,50–52 Union St, London, SW1 1TD (tel: 020 7593 1700, www.hillsbalfour.com).

US and Canada: Tourist information can be obtained from the Mauritius Embassy, Suite 441, 4301 Connecticut Avenue NW, Washington DC 20008 (tel: 202 244 1491/92, https://mauritius-washington.govmu.org).

In Mauritius, the main MTPA office is on the 4–5th floor, Victoria House, St Louis Street, Port Louis (tel: 230 203 1900, www.mymauritius.travel). A tourist information kiosk is inside the SSR International Airport arrivals hall (tel: 230 637 3635). Rodrigues' tourist office is in Port Mathurin (tel: 230 832 0866). They also have a handy app, Discover Rodrigues, with a map, accommodation, excursions and contacts.

TRANSPORT

Buses. Buses are provided by dozens of bus companies, individual owners and co-operative societies. They are reliable, cheap and plentiful, even if some are rather dilapidated and slow. During the week, they are crowded from 8am to 9am and 4pm to 5pm, but at other times, bus travel can be a pleasant experience and a way of rubbing shoulders with local people. Port Louis has two bus stations: Immigration Square, serving the north, and Victoria Square, serving the plateau towns and the south. Fares range between R30 and R50 or up to R100 if travelling by air-conditioned express service. Conductors will balk at notes, so always carry small changes. Queues are orderly and you buy your ticket on board.

Buses operate in the resorts from 6.30am to 6.30pm and elsewhere from 5.30am to 8pm, with the last bus leaving at 11pm from Port Louis to Curepipe via the plateau towns. The main carrier is the National Transport Corporation (CNT) (tel: 230 427 5000, www.buscnt.mu), with offices in bus stations around the island and a handy route finder.

Taxis. Taxis are not metered. Although tariffs are regulated and a tariff card should be displayed, agreeing on a price before accepting a journey is customary. Licensed taxis can be hired from taxi stands in town and outside most hotels, or ask your receptionist. The hotels have a special arrangement with the drivers, who are expected to charge reasonable rates. If you feel you are being overcharged, warn the driver that you will report him to the hotel. This strategy normally works.

Taxis are recognisable by black registration numbers on white plates, while those belonging to hotels will have the hotel's name emblazoned clearly on their door. Avoid the unlicensed taxis (*taxis marrons*), which are instantly recognisable because they are nothing more than private cars with white numbers on black plates. Rates may be low, but they are not insured to carry passengers. Taxis can be hired for a full or half day and can be cheaper and certainly more convenient than hiring a car to drive yourself.

Taxicab Mauritius (www.taxicabmauritius.com) and Taxis Mauritius (www. taxismauritius.com) are reputable companies that display their rates online. If you want to travel like a local, another option is shared taxis which ply the routes around and between main towns. They are inexpensive as the fare is shared between the passengers. Look for them in the main areas (or ask the locals). They wait until they fill up, which is usually not long. If you want to take a piece of luggage, you'll probably need to pay for an extra seat.

V

VISAS AND ENTRY REQUIREMENTS

Nationals of the EU, USA and all Commonwealth countries do not need visas. Your passport should be valid for six months beyond your arrival date. Entry is usually for a maximum of three months and you will be asked for your return or onward ticket and to provide an address in Mauritius. For more extended stays, you should go in person to the Immigration Department, Sterling House, 9-11 Lislet Geoffroy St, Port Louis (tel: 230 260 2073, https://passport.govmu.org/passport). You will need two passport-size photographs, valid return tickets and evidence of funds to support your stay.

Prescription medicines for personal use carried in an official container are permitted. Finally, anyone trying to engage in drug trafficking will likely find themselves in jail for a long time.

W

WEBSITES

There are a number of valuable websites giving information for people intending to visit Mauritius:

www.pawsmauritius.org – animal welfare charity working to reduce the stray dog population through mass sterilization programmes and adoption.

www.mauritian-wildlife.org – conservation NGO for information on Mauritian and Rodriguan flora and fauna.

http://metservice.intnet.mu – the official meteorological site for Mauritius.

https://govmu.org – official government website.

www.expat.com/en/destination/africa/mauritius – informative community site with an extensive network of expatriates

www.otayo.com – for what's on the local cultural scene.

www.islandinfo.mu – an online magazine with cultural articles and local listings.

WHERE TO STAY

Although internationally branded hotels are present on the island, some of the most stylish accommodation in the best locations is owned and managed by major Mauritian hotel companies, such as Beachcomber, Sunlife, Ninety-Six Hotel Collection (formerly Indigo Hotels), Veranda Resorts, Attitude and The LUX Collective. Most offer the option of an all-inclusive stay, bookable through your home travel agent or tour operator.

The following guide indicates prices for a double room with breakfast during the low season. A higher price rating does not necessarily mean that accommodation and service are superior but has more to do with the number of facilities and proximity and access to exceptionally well-maintained beaches. Locally known as *pieds dans l'eau* (meaning 'feet in the water'), these properties command higher prices than those a few blocks inland. Remember to add 15 percent VAT when budgeting for your accommodation.

$$$$	over R15,000
$$$	R10,000–15,000
$$	R5,000–10,000
$	below R5,000

PORT LOUIS

Labourdonnais Waterfront Hotel $$$$ *Caudan Waterfront, tel: 230 202 4000,* www.ninetysixhotels.com/labourdonnais-waterfront-hotel-port-louis-mauritius.html. Port Louis' flagship business-class hotel, named after the founder of the capital, Bertrand François Mahé de La Bourdonnais, hogs the best position on the waterfront. The tastefully decorated rooms have gorgeous mountain and harbour views. Its open-door policy attracts non-residents to its two restaurants and elegant Post Box bar.

Le Saint Georges Hotel $$ *19 Rue St Georges, tel: 230 211 2581,* www.saint georgeshotel-mu.com. Unpretentious eighty-room hotel with a small pool in a quiet part of the city appealing to short-stay business and leisure travellers. The simple restaurant serves Creole and European fare and has a pub-style bar.

Le Suffren Hotel & Marina $$$ *Caudan Waterfront, tel: 230 202 4900*, www.ninetysixhotels.com/le-suffren-hotel-and-marina-port-louis-mauritius.html. Named after a French admiral, this recently-renovated 102-room hotel has a distinct nautical atmosphere, with a swimming pool and artificial beach giving views over the capital and a spa. Its trendy bar and two a la carte restaurants attract a hip Friday night crowd. Complimentary beach trips and water taxi to its sister hotel, the Labourdonnais, plus next door to Odysseo Oceanarium.

THE NORTH

Le Palmiste Resort & Spa $$ *Trou aux Biches, tel: 230 265 6815*, https://sites.google.com/view/le-palmiste-resort-spa. Popular with independent travellers and tour groups. Pleasant, simple accommodation, only a five-minute walk from the beach. Buffet restaurant and three pools; holistic treatments are available in the spa.

Paradise Cove Boutique Hotel $$$$ *Anse La Raie, tel: 230 204 3820*, www.paradisecovehotel.com. Small and luxurious couples retreat in a remote location with an infinity pool overlooking Coin de Mire Island. Romantic a la carte seafood restaurant, spa and gorgeous private white cove. Popular with honeymooners. Dive centre.

The Oberoi Beach Resort $$$$ *Turtle Bay, Pointe aux Piments, tel: 230 204 3600*, www.oberoihotels.com. A small, elegant and highly sophisticated place, strictly the preserve of honeymooners and the occasional A-list celebrity seeking absolute calm. Superbly furnished individual villas, some with plunge pools and high-walled outdoor bathrooms, guarantee privacy. The open-sided silver-service restaurant overlooks a white sandy beach, and Balinese-style statues adorn two pools.

Trou aux Biches Beachcomber Golf Resort & Spa $$$$ *Royal Road, Trou aux Biches, Triolet, tel: 230 204 6800*, www.beachcomber-hotels.com. This village-style all-suite and villa resort with plenty of pools and six restaurants on a great stretch of powder-white sand. Good choice for honeymooners, empty nesters and families with young children.

Veranda Grand Baie $$ *Grand Baie, tel: 230 209 8000*, www.veranda-resorts.com. Inspired by typical Creole guesthouses, this cosy colonial-style ocean-fronted hideaway reopened after a complete renovation in July 2023. Choice of twenty apartments with kitchenette, plus 74 well-equipped standard rooms, poolside dining, a spa, and local activities.

Veranda Paul et Virginie $$ *Coast Road, Grand Gaube, tel: 230 209 2400*, www.veranda-resorts.com. All-inclusive options and an authentic colonial atmosphere make this adult-only hotel a firm favourite with European couples. Two infinity pools, a fine seafood restaurant on the jetty, an intimate bar and 81 comfortable sea-facing rooms.

Villas Mon Plaisir $ *Royal Road, Pointe aux Piments, tel: 230 261 7471*, www.villasmonplaisir.com. This charming family-run complex of 48 two-storey units set in pleasant gardens with a pool is situated on the edge of the village and right on the beach. Welcoming restaurant and bar. Free watersports and dive centre.

Zilwa Attitude $$ *Royal Road, Calodyne, tel: 230 204 9800*, http://hotels-attitude.com/en/zilwa-attitude. In Creole, 'zilwa' means 'islander'. The hotel was designed with the aim of sharing the simple and genuine life of islanders with its guests and boasts an inspiring view of Coin de Mire. Six themed restaurants offer delicious cuisine, and it has four pools and a spa. Popular with families, couples and newlyweds.

THE EAST

LUX Belle Mare $$$$ *Belle Mare Plage, tel: 230 402 2000*, www.luxresorts.com. The reinvented LUX Belle Mare reopens on 1 October 2023 as an eminently chic retreat appealing to honeymooners, couples and families. The aperitif bar and new gourmet Indian and Chinese restaurants overlook a gorgeous pool and kilometre of beach. A wonderful spa, nightly entertainment, complimentary watersports and kids- and teens-club round out the picture.

Constance Belle Mare Plage $$$$ *Belle Mare Plage, tel: 230 402 2600*, www.constancehotels.com. This large, well-established hotel has benefited from regular refurbishment. Luxurious villas with private plunge pools, suites or standard rooms are set in lush gardens with swimming pools and sea views. Free watersports, dive centre, mini-club for 4–11-year-olds, two championship 18-hole golf courses, eight a la carte restaurants – including one in a wine cellar - and spa provide everything you need for an active beach holiday.

Friday Attitude $$$ *Trou d'Eau Douce, tel: 230 402 7070*, www.friday-hotel-mauritius.com. Go for personal attention and local flavour rather than a prestigious address at this all-inclusive boutique haven where you can use the same beach as many grander hotels. Freshly furnished rooms, swimming pool, spa, intimate restaurants and bars, and a kid's club for 3- to 12-year-olds.

La Hacienda $ *Lion Mountain, Vieux Grand Port, tel. 230 5989 1866,* www.laciendamauritius.com. Situated on the side of the mountain in the historic region of Old Grand Port near Mahébourg, with views over the large bay, the sea and the southeast islands. La Hacienda contains four unique guest houses, surrounded by private gardens with a communal pool and eco-activities.

Long Beach Mauritius $$$$ *Belle Mare, tel: 230 401 1919*, www.longbeachmauritius.com. This large, contemporary beach resort with restaurants, shops and bars around a piazza lies on a beautiful kilometre of powder-white sand. It's chic and sporty (with everything from a lap pool to a climbing wall) and its 'Come Alive' experiences include medicinal cocktails at the sprawling spa.

Preskil Island Resort $$$ *Pointe Jerome, Mahébourg, tel: 230 604 1000*, https://southerncrosshotels.mu. This Creole chic hotel under thatch has a superb location with views of Lion Mountain and Île aux Aigrettes Nature Reserve. Popular with groups, it is only a fifteen-minute drive from the airport, with contemporary restaurants. Freshly renovated garden rooms and sea-facing cottages in warm colours contrast with a trio of powdery white beaches.

SALT of Palmar $$ *Coastal Road, Palmar, tel: 230 401 8500*, www.saltresorts.com. This arty adult-only boutique hotel on the untamed east coast was the first eco-hotel on the island and has a local vibe. A rooftop bar, creative food – with vegan options, and eye-popping murals by Camille Walala attract fashionistas and honeymooners. Focusing on meaningful travel, it offers original experiences, from a trip to the southeast islands with a Mahébourg local to a soulful hike learning the mysteries of Le Morne Mountain.

THE SOUTH

Heritage Awali Golf & Spa Resort $$$$ *Bel Ombre, tel: 230 260 5101*, www.heritageresorts.mu. Lots of in-house activities and free shuttle trips to the nearby nature reserve and an 18-hole golf course compensate for the isolation of this premium, all-inclusive luxury hotel. Distinct Creole-African theme with large thatched-roof restaurants and bars, two fine pools, a spa and baby, kids and teens club.

Heritage Le Telfair Golf & Wellness Resort $$$$ *Bel Ombre, tel: 230 260 5101*, www.heritageresorts.mu. This unique masterpiece of grand colonial-inspired architecture transports guests to an atmosphere of refinement and calm. Rooms have floor-to-ceiling windows with private balconies, and suites have butlers. Luxuriant gardens, five restaurants (one with show kitchen) and bars, including a beach club, wellness pavilion, baby, kids club and teen programme and unlimited golf. Guests can alternate between swimming in the lagoon and exploring the undulating hills of the Bel Ombre Nature Reserve.

La Vieille Cheminee $$ *Chamarel, tel: 230 483 4249*, www.lavieillecheminee.com. Close to the 7 Coloured Earth, these charmingly rustic self-catering chalet bungalows on a tropical farm in the Chamarel highlands offer a chance to explore rural Mauritius. There are horse riding, cycling and trekking opportunities, and dining in nearby village restaurants. A two- or three-day stay here is an unusual alternative to the sun, sea and sand – although it's only a twenty-minute drive away.

Otentic Eco Tent Experience $$ *Deux Frères, tel: 230 5841 4888*, https://otentic.mu. This friendly, laid-back glamping site with twelve safari tents overlooking Grand Riviere Sud-Est offers communal dining, a rainwater pool, and eco-activities. A boat ferries guests to Ile aux Cerfs for swimming in the mornings; then there's sea and river kayaking, stand-up paddle boarding, hiking and off-road biking in the sugar fields and mountains, and superb Mauritian food. A bus stop at the top of the drive takes you into historic Mahébourg.

Sofitel So Mauritius $$$$ *Royal Road, Bel Ombre, tel: 230 605 5800*, https://sofitel.accor.com. A fantastic oasis boasting lush vegetation and a beautiful lagoon. The designs of Kenzo Takada enhanced Thai architect Lek Bunnag's project here. Elegant and sophisticated, with attentive service, suites and villas. Well-being and spa service are available.

THE WEST

Maradiva Villas Resort & Spa $$$$ *Wolmar, Flic en Flac, tel: 203 403 1500*. www.maradiva.com. A sprawling complex of luxurious villas set in tropical gardens with a long stretch of beach overlooking Tamarin Mountain, which was completely renovated in 2023 (reopening 31st Oct). Fine dining options, a kids' club and a beautiful Ayurvedic spa. It's a honeymoon favourite.

Paradis Beachcomber Golf Resort & Spa $$$$ *Le Morne Peninsula, tel: 230 401 5050*, www.beachcomber-hotels.com. Paradis Beachcomber is a haven for sports and nature lovers and was refurbished in 2023 (it reopens in mid-October). As well as bars and restaurants, the resort includes a championship 18-hole golf course against a mountain backdrop and offers deep-sea fishing, diving, mountain biking, a kids club for 3- to 11-year-olds and an atmospheric spa.

Sands Suites Resort & Spa $$$$ *Wolmar, Flic en Flac, tel: 230 403 1200*, www.sands.mu. A discreet, serene and sophisticated all-suite beach hotel with beautiful views of the Tamarin Mountains. Ideal for empty nesters and honeymooners. Three fine restaurants, a spa and huge swimming pool, and access to golf nearby.

Sugar Beach Resort $$$$ *Wolmar, Flic en Flac, tel: 230 403 3300*, www.sugarbeachresort.com. Sunlife's recently-renovated cool, white and spacious resort is reminiscent of colonial times, but with all mod cons, nightly entertainment and the island's largest swimming pool. Enjoy high tea in the palatial nineteenth-century-style sugar plantation manor house, play croquet on the lawn or have a beauty treatment in the beach bubble.

Veranda Tamarin Hotel $$ *Tamarin Bay, tel: 230 483 4313,* www.veranda-resorts.com. Conveniently situated close to the village and in front of the curve of Tamarin Bay, this cosy, convivial hotel with a surfy vibe attracts young couples and families. Facilities include a rooftop restaurant, kids club, Seven Colours spa, a long rectangular swimming pool, a surf shop and a boathouse. Island activities are offered through an explorer programme, and guests can mingle with residents at the Crazy Fish bar, with entertainment by local musicians.

Villas Caroline $$ *Coast Road, Flic en Flac, tel: 230 453 8411,* https://villas carolinehotel.com. Attractive, well-maintained complex, with rooms in red-roofed Creole-colonial buildings, overlooking a brilliant white spit of sand within walking distance of restaurants and bars. Superb dive school, a wide range of water sports, friendly service, and a pool and spa.

PLATEAU TOWNS

Hennessy Park Hotel $$ *65 Ebène Cybercity, Ebèn, tel: 230 403 7200,* https://ninetysixhotels.com. Contemporary and artistic business-class hotel with all the mod cons, such as a gym, spa and eclectic restaurants, including Japanese. The lively clientele spend weekends in the Backstage bar and chilling at an alfresco rooftop pool bar. Convenient access to Port Louis.

RODRIGUES

Cotton Bay Resort & Spa $$$ *Pointe Coton, tel: 230 831 8001,* www.cotton bayresortandspa.com. Comfortable hotel with refreshed rooms in a superbly isolated beach location. Excellent dive centre with diving right on the doorstep and access to glorious coastal walks.

Escale Vacances $$ *Fond La Digue, Port Mathurin, tel: 230 5251 1153,* www.escale-vacances.com. A five-minute walk from the town centre, this well-established Creole-style hotel has a cosy family atmosphere and an excellent restaurant.

PLAY Mourouk Hotel $$$ *Pate Reynieux, Port Sud-Est, tel: 230 832 3351*, www.playmourouk.com. This iconic hotel in a cliff-top location, with its distinctive red rooftops, was completely renovated and upgraded in 2023. It offers attractive bungalow-style accommodation in Creole colonial architecture with a boathouse, dive school and kite surfing.

Tekoma Boutik Hotel $$$ *Anse Ally, tel: 230 831 8810*, www.tekoma-hotel.com. This small hotel with a trendy vibe has 32 rooms in individual chalets, including five beachfront suites, all with a sea view from the terrace overlooking Saint-Francois Bay. It's in a fabulous location, and facilities include an outdoor pool, a beach club, a panoramic restaurant and bar, a diving centre and a spa.

INDEX

THE **MINI** ROUGH GUIDE TO
MAURITIUS & RODRIGUES

First Edition 2023

Editor: Sarah Clark
Author: Nicki Grihault
Picture Editor: Tom Smyth
Cartography Update: Carte
Layout: Greg Madejak
Head of DTP and Pre-Press: Rebeka Davies
Head of Publishing: Sarah Clark
Photography Credits: Beachcomber Hotels
40; Corbis 53; Fotoseeker 49; Getty Images
75, 77, 78, 81; iStock 6T, 6B, 11, 14, 15, 38, 69,
101; Le Sultan 7T, 98; MTPA 7B, 13, 26, 28, 32,
35, 38, 44, 51, 56, 59, 63, 70, 84, 87, 88, 91, 92,
99, 100, 103, 107; Public domain 17, 18, 20, 23;
Shutterstock 1, 4TL, 4TC, 4TR, 4CL, 4CR, 4BL,
4BR, 5T, 5C, 5B, 31, 36, 43, 47, 54, 61, 64, 67,
73, 82, 95, 105
Cover Credits: Beach and Le Morne Brabant
Vaclav Volrab/Shutterstock

Distribution
UK, Ireland and Europe: Apa Publications (UK)
Ltd; sales@roughguides.com
United States and Canada: Ingram Publisher
Services; ips@ingramcontent.com
Australia and New Zealand: Booktopia;
retailer@booktopia.com.au
Worldwide: Apa Publications (UK) Ltd;
sales@roughguides.com

**Special Sales, Content Licensing
and CoPublishing**
Rough Guides can be purchased in bulk
quantities at discounted prices. We can create
special editions, personalised jackets and
corporate imprints tailored to your needs.
sales@roughguides.com; http://roughguides.com

All Rights Reserved
© 2023 Apa Digital AG
License edition © Apa Publications Ltd UK

Printed in Czech Republic

This book was produced using **Typefi** automated
publishing software.

Contact us
Every effort has been made to provide accurate
information in this publication, but changes
are inevitable. The publisher cannot be held
responsible for any resulting loss, inconvenience
or injury sustained by any traveller as a result of
information or advice contained in the guide.
We would appreciate it if readers would call our
attention to any errors or outdated information, or if
you feel we've left something out. Please send your
comments with the subject line "Rough Guide Mini
Mauritius Update" to mail@uk.roughguides.com.